Awestruck by
WORDSTRUCK

"MacNeil writes of his family with charm and poignancy . . . but it is when he writes about English that MacNeil is at his best."
—*Chicago Tribune*

"A charming memoir . . . In its best pages one can almost whiff the salty tang of fog descending on proud, poky Halifax as winter comes."
—*Time*

"MacNeil comments perceptively on many aspects of our changing culture. . . ."
—*The Cleveland Plain Dealer*

"MacNeil's writing made me want to rush to savor again works as varied as *Winnie-the-Pooh* and the poems of T. S. Eliot."
—*New York Woman*

"Deftly woven into this warm life story is a history of the English language. . . . MacNeil is ever interested, relevant, and surprisingly playful. This is a lovely memoir."
—*7 Days*

"If you love words . . . you'll appreciate *Wordstruck*."
—*Houston Chronicle*

"This account is witty, deep, scholarly, sensuous—and endlessly interesting."
—*St. Petersburg Times*

"Because this warm and evocative memoir . . . reverberates with the love of words, of books, of poetry, of the theatre—of the sound of English—it should become a classic to all who are wordstruck."
—Stuart Flexner, author of *Listening to America*

PENGUIN BOOKS

WORDSTRUCK

Robert MacNeil is co-anchor and executive editor
of the MacNeil/Lehrer NewsHour. He is the
co-author of the bestselling
The Story of English.

WORDSTRUCK

A MEMOIR

Robert MacNeil

PENGUIN BOOKS

PENGUIN BOOKS
Published by the Penguin Group
Viking Penguin, a division of Penguin Books USA Inc.,
40 West 23rd Street, New York, New York 10010, U.S.A.
Penguin Books Ltd, 27 Wrights Lane, London W8 5TZ, England
Penguin Books Australia Ltd, Ringwood, Victoria, Australia
Penguin Books Canada Ltd, 2801 John Street, Markham, Ontario, Canada L3R 1B4
Penguin Books (N.Z.) Ltd, 182–190 Wairau Road, Auckland 10, New Zealand

Penguin Books Ltd, Registered Offices: Harmondsworth, Middlesex, England

First published in the United States of America by
Viking Penguin, a division of Penguin Books USA Inc., 1989
Published in Penguin Books 1990

1   3   5   7   9   10   8   6   4   2

Grateful acknowledgment is made for permission to reprint excerpts from the following copyrighted works:
"Der Führer's Face," by Oliver Wallace. Copyright 1942 by Southern Music Publishing Co., Inc.; copyright renewed.
"The White Cliffs of Dover," by Nat Burton and Walter Kent. © 1941 by Shapiro, Bernstein & Co., Inc. Copyright renewed by Shapiro, Bernstein & Co. and Kent Music Company. Used by permission.
"Little Gidding," from Four Quartets, by T. S. Eliot. Copyright 1943 by T. S. Eliot, renewed 1971 by Esme Valerie Eliot. Reprinted by permission of Harcourt Brace Jovanovich, Inc., and Faber and Faber Ltd.
"The Love Song of J. Alfred Prufrock" and "The Waste Land," from Collected Poems 1909–1962, by T. S. Eliot. Copyright 1936 by Harcourt Brace Jovanovich, Inc., copyright © 1963, 1964 by T. S. Eliot. Reprinted by permission of Harcourt Brace Jovanovich, Inc., and Faber and Faber Ltd.
"Do not go gentle into that good night" and "In the White Giant's Thigh," from Poems of Dylan Thomas. Copyright 1952 by Dylan Thomas. Reprinted by permission of New Directions Publishing Corporation. Published in Great Britain by J. M. Dent & Sons Ltd.

Photographs from the author's collection.

LIBRARY OF CONGRESS CATALOGING IN PUBLICATION DATA
MacNeil, Robert, 1931–
Wordstruck: a memoir/Robert MacNeil.
p.   cm.
Reprint. Originally published: New York, N.Y.: Viking, 1989.
ISBN 0 14 01.0401 1
1. MacNeil, Robert, 1931–   —Childhood and youth.
2. Philologists—United States—Biography.   3. Journalists—United
States—Biography.   4. Nova Scotia—Social life and customs.
5. English language—Style.   6. Books and reading.   I. Title.
[PE64.M23A3   1990]
070′.92—dc20
[B]   89–39517

Printed in the United States of America   ·   Set in Oldstyle No. 7

*This book is dedicated
to my children,
Cathy, Ian, Alison, and Will,
with my love and
admiration.*

PREFACE

For several years recently I worked with others on a television series and a book, *The Story of English*. For all of us it was a labour of love, so that we were surprised along the way to encounter people who considered the language a dull subject, or thought they did until they saw the series or read the book. It was evident that many people did not know that the language was something they could love. My experience was so different that I began thinking about it and this book is the result.

When Jim Lehrer read it, he said: "You should call it *Wordstruck* because that is what you were." Wordstruck is exactly what I was—and still am: crazy about the sound of words, the look of words, the taste of words, the feeling for words on the tongue and in the mind.

This is the story of how it happened to me; how I became wordstruck.

CHAPTER ONE

*I*t is a winter's night in 1936 in Halifax, Nova Scotia. A small boy is being read to. He is warm from a hot bath, wearing striped flannel pyjamas and a thick woollen dressing gown with a tasselled cord. He has dropped off his slippers to slide his bare feet between the cushions of the sofa.

Outside, a salty wind blows snow against the panes of the windows. It sifts under the front door and through the three ventilation holes in the storm windows, creating tiny drifts. Foghorns are grumping far in the distance. The coal fire in the basket grate burns intense and silent. His mother reads:

> Whenever the moon and stars are set,
>   Whenever the wind is high,
> All night long in the dark and wet,
>   A man goes riding by.
> Late in the night when the fires are out,
> Why does he gallop and gallop about?

Probably thinking of her husband, the boy's father, somewhere out at sea on such a night, she reads:

> Whenever the trees are crying aloud,
>   And ships are tossed at sea,

By, on the highway, low and loud,
  By at the gallop goes he.
By at the gallop he goes and then,
  By he comes at the gallop again.

There wasn't a fire every night. Some fireplaces burned wood and some coal. The coal fire might have been a few years later. All of those things happened often but I cannot remember whether they happened all at one time. It might have been spring with the liquid warble of an evening bird, echoing in the damp green air outside, like sounds intimate in a fog; or a long evening in summer with bees buzzing against screens and a chickadee plaintive in the distance. Often I was in bed when read to, pleading for a few more pages before going to sleep, or sick and listening lethargically. But in memory it feels like a winter night. What I remember precisely is the reading; both what was read and what I felt about it.

"Windy Nights" by Robert Louis Stevenson still makes my breath come a little quicker, gives me the scary, yet exciting, feeling that outside in the dark there are things to be feared—but adventure too.

What was it that made me captive to those first words? I have been snooping around in my childhood, trying to pick up the clues, to find the trail. Some of it must have come from the way the words were read, and where, and when.

Although I was born in Montreal, it was in Halifax that I learned to talk and later to read and write. So it was as a Nova Scotian that I joined the English-speaking peoples: my first English came flavoured with a salty tang and with odd names for things, like *chesterfield* for sofa. The time guaranteed a pre-television childhood in strict schools, where mere cleanliness was not as close to godliness as good grammar.

My parents loved books, and the Depression left them too hard up for much other diversion. My mother would weep over a book, my father lose himself in one for hours.

All this combined to fashion a childhood which made words important. Pleasure was another matter. The pleasures of children were not as aggressively consulted—or exploited—then as now; the child as a consumer had yet to be invented. I did not consciously come to love the language, and to know I did, until much later, until late adolescence. But in these years all the seeds of love were planted.

The words were spoken into my ears by my Nova Scotian mother, in a musical voice which inclined towards British intonations. It was not an English accent; it was cultured Haligonian, a variety of the distinctive, close-lipped Nova Scotian dialect. It was multi-hued, like glass fused of many bottles in a fire, with wisps of Lowland Scots and Highland Gaelic, Irish, Hanoverian German, Acadian French, and the many flavours of English deposited by generations of British soldiers and sailors. My mother's words sounded Nova Scotian, but the lilt and music of the speech—its rise and fall and its rhythms—were English. My father's speech, acquired in Montreal, was more flatly Canadian. He was the constant reader and collector of books, but for much of my childhood he was away at sea. It was my mother who read to me and my two younger brothers.

She read with enthusiasm and delight. If reading the childish stories bored her, she never showed it. She sounded as enthralled, as full of wonder and close-rivetted attention as I was. She had a sense of dramatic situation and character and played the parts to the hilt. She felt the descriptive passages and gave them full value; the uplifting and poetic moments got a reading worthy of them.

My mother was a singer of some talent and knew enough

French from her school days in Switzerland to teach a little in Halifax. Both activities made her very conscious of diction. She spoke with precise enunciation herself and was constantly at us to do the same.

"Enunciate your vowels," she was always saying, "enunciate your vowels," in the way her father, Dr. Oxner, the dentist, said, "Masticate your food—masticate your food," and his wife, Daisy Oxner, would ask dramatically, "Have you moved your bowels?" These admonitions all took on the same moral colouring to me and played like mantras through my early years:

"Have you moved your bowels?"

"Masticate your food!"

"Enunciate your vowels!"

My parents—Peggy and Bob, or Bobby and Peg, as they were variously known—had tastes that exceeded their ability to indulge them. Like many people then, they were not poor but members of the large, scraping middle classes. We lived nicely, sometimes helped by their families, but in a way that would seem deprived today: rented apartments, no car, an icebox not a refrigerator.

They had fun. Two of the first non-baby words I uttered were *gin fizz*, mysteriously the name of a large blue teddy bear, a favour they brought back from a New Year's Eve party. Gin Fizz was my companion for years, my Winnie-the-Pooh. Because of him, I believed Christopher Robin's bear was blue. My parents claimed that I named him Gin Fizz; that might say something about their life style, but I cannot remember. I did not know it was a drink for years, and by the time I found out, no one drank it any more. The French called a line of yachts Gin Fizz, for equally obscure reasons. For me the words never connoted anything but teddy bear.

My father girded himself with romantic dreams, fed by con-

stant reading, of becoming a writer like Hemingway, or ful-
filling himself in some dashing, worldly way. He was born with
a big, confident spirit, and my mother, when not agonising
about money, shared his dreams.

In each of their family's past were grand things: on her side,
through Neelys and Breckenridges, the American Revolution
and the Civil War; on his, the Wares of Harvard. My mother's
grandfather, a Colonel John Breckenridge Neely, fought with
Tennessee for the Confederacy; my father's great-uncle Robert
Ware was killed while serving as a surgeon in the Union Army.
On my mother's side were Quakers and Presbyterians, on my
father's Unitarian theologians and Episcopalians. In the wonderful untidiness of North American life, two of these Americans drifted into Canadian marriages which produced my
mother and father. Enriching the gene pool were German
farmer-fishermen, poor Scots crofters, a family of Irish actors
and theater managers, and a whispered assortment of drunk-
ards, wastrels, and charming ne'er-do-wells. Since neither of
my parents shrank from imagining grandeur revived, they
loaded their first-born, me, with two middle names, Breckenridge Ware.

How they looked the part when they were young! Well-bred,
as they would have put it, handsome in clothes, my father with
a matinee idol's profile without the sleaze; my mother's oval
face and thin figure perfect for the cloche hats and low-waisted
clothes of the twenties. In the faded photographs of their al-
bums, he poses, dashing, in a blazer with tennis racket, she in
hiking gear in the Swiss Alps, or having tea on a lawn by the
sea, wearing dark lipstick and shiny silk stockings. They could
have been an advertisement for anything of the period. They
were confident of their manners, proud of their families, and
unstintingly optimistic about the future.

He came to Halifax and noticed her in the street. He kept asking who she was, until he learned that her father was a dentist, Warren Oxner, with offices in his house on Spring Garden Road, opposite where the Lord Nelson Hotel stands today. With a pin my father picked a filling out of a tooth to have an excuse to see Dr. Oxner. My mother loved to tell the story: "That's the kind of man Bob was. Daddy was so taken with him that he invited him to dinner.

"He could charm a bird off a tree. I never met anyone with such a gift of the gab. There must be more Irish in him than he pretends. His mother is just the same and his father was one of the most courtly old gentlemen I've ever met. Where did they get their manners from?"

He was away so much that she talked about him constantly, often forgetting that I was there, waiting with a dish towel to dry the next dish, while she told me over and over again, sometimes happily, sometimes weeping into the dishpan, how they met, how he dazzled her into an engagement and a marriage.

"Bob could talk his way into anything or out of anything" was often the cue line.

A woman alone, or alone with small children, becomes a monologist, often not really talking to the children but using their presence to unbutton her feelings.

Those were other words I heard first—the story of their lives, her version of history, which moved as slowly and as repetitively as a soap opera, with as many heartbreaks. The words of her own stories, and of the stories she read me, were the first words I drank in.

Children have difficulty seeing their parents as sexual creatures, yet I think I inferred long before I knew any of the literal facts how she longed for him physically, how passionate they were.

My father sailing in 1928,
the year before his marriage

She was less diffident in talking about it than he, but they were both sensual people, who touched, smelled, heard, and tasted hungrily, under the veneer of good manners. They were lively and adventurous: both risk-takers, with itchy feet and wanderlust; each steeped in the proprieties, but each with a tiny urge to kick over authority.

They got engaged by the sea, picnicking in the coves near Halifax, Modesty Cove and, appropriately, Peggy's Cove, now one of the most photographed beauty spots in Canada, then just a fishing village. Frank Wright, a friend of my father's, was with them: "It was very hot that night—so hot that you couldn't sit on the rocks, and the water was so cold that you couldn't stay in. So the three of us, Peg and Bob and I, kept jumping in and out like seals. The moonlight was very bright. Bob and Peg disappeared and when they came back they were engaged."

They were married on September 28, 1929. Thirty-one days later, the stock market and their world crashed: their life together began with the Great Depression. They had married on the strength of his job as a travelling representative for Essex cars. The job disappeared: within a month, the company died and the brand became extinct.

"He literally walked the streets for three years, looking for work," my mother often said, "three years, in such despair. You can't imagine what it was like. We lost our little flat. We couldn't manage the rent."

It was part of her good manners not to use crude, direct words like *pay the rent* but to soften the thought with a word like *manage*. People were not *rich* but *well off*, not *poor* but *hard up*. The nice way of saying they were *broke* was: "We

My mother in 1929,
at the time of her engagement

hadn't a sou in the world. We had to move to Montreal because more seemed to be happening there. But the streets were full of men like your dad, desperate for anything. The second Christmas, Mother and Daddy sent us a Christmas dinner from Halifax by train, in a hamper—everything, even the crackers and cranberry sauce." That always made her cry.

"He would do anything. The first summer after you were born, the summer of 1931, they were hiring men at Beauharnois, the big construction project on the St. Lawrence. Your father carried water for the construction workers. He carried buckets of water! But so did lots of men with college degrees and he didn't have a degree."

In the small cottage they found at Beauharnois, he was also trying to write, following a correspondence course from London. Although they were scraping for pennies that summer, he bought the newly published *Foundations of English Prose* by A. C. Ward, marking especially the essentials of short-story writing.

After one year, I became very ill with a digestive disorder called celiac, which no one knew how to treat. My father carried me on foot to the hospital, where I spent most of the next two years. I got so sick that he had to give me a direct blood transfusion through veins in my ankles.

That shelved the writing dream. At the end of 1933, worn out by his hopeless job search, he joined the Royal Canadian Mounted Police as a recruit. My mother's relief was tinged with embarrassment. No one she knew entered any service "in the ranks," but as officers. In the RCMP, you had to start in the ranks. She was not a snob but a girl used to young Army and naval officers as beaux, and now the husbands of her friends. It made a big social difference.

With a background of sailing as a sea scout and a love of the sea, my father entered the Mounties not on horseback but in a ship. In the Marine Section, forerunner of Canada's Coast Guard, his abilities brought extraordinary advancement. Within four years he had a Master's Ticket and was skipper of an RCMP patrol boat. On winter nights, when my mother was reading to me, he was having daring adventures in the foggy seas off Nova Scotia and Newfoundland. Their biggest job was chasing the "rum-runners" who smuggled booze from the Caribbean and the French islands of St. Pierre and Miquelon to bootleggers in Nova Scotia.

To satisfy some of his writing urge he vividly described this work in articles for the *RCMP Quarterly* and that attracted the attention of headquarters in Ottawa.

When Canada declared war on Germany on September 10, 1939, sea experience like Dad's was in short supply. He and his ship, *Laurier,* were commissioned into the Canadian Navy. For the rest of the war, he was away commanding a series of warships—two corvettes, a destroyer, and a frigate—in the Battle of the Atlantic. From the time I was three, in 1934, until the war ended in 1945, he was at home only for brief periods and my mother was effectively the parent.

Whatever he was doing, his books were a constant; even when he was short of cash for anything else, like paying bills, books appeared. In fact, he used books to hide the bills he couldn't pay. Occasionally I found little nests of them when I pulled out a book. My mother said scornfully that was Irish— dealing with unpleasant reality by putting it away somewhere, out of mind. She never knew which books to look behind. It made her both furious with him and tender.

He always wrote on the flyleaf of each new book the date and where he was, so I can follow him: reading Chesterton just after they were married in November 1929, Scottish poets the following spring, Conrad through the early thirties, and Proust at sea in wartime—*Swann's Way,* 1941, in HMCS *Dauphin; Within a Budding Grove,* in 1944, aboard HMCS *Columbia.* Some books spent the war in sea bags and still show it. There were always books and they were moved each time we moved. His brother, Corty, an artist, designed bookplates, and after the war, my father spent weeks pasting them into his books. He treated the bindings of his leatherbound books with oil to keep them supple. He loved the feel of books, good paper, well-sewn bindings; while still a small child I was hearing about half-calf and morocco bindings.

He acquired the three-volume Oxford Shakespeare in large type on India paper with gilded edges. He would take one volume down, make me feel the tissue-thin paper, and remark how the binding fell flat open. He made them seem delicious, like something good enough to eat. He promised, and reminded me very often, that they would be mine one day, as they are.

His books formed a permanent and always expanding part of the furniture, and therefore interior decoration, of our homes. Their spines grew deeply familiar, like patterns in a wallpaper, only more constant because we moved quite often.

Reading was the affordable cheap entertainment of those times, and in my mother's phrase, my father "always had his nose buried in a book." It was his escape, his dream space, his wish-fulfillment, the travel of a man who yearned to travel more, and his higher education. He provided his own college, as Churchill did, by reading himself through Western culture. Encountering the range of his books today, I am impressed with how much wider his reading went in some directions than mine has. He had the classics in translation. He revered the English poets, had them all, and read them regularly. He gave me *The Oxford Book of English Verse* when I was fifteen and a copy of *Ulysses* at eighteen, as though they were pieces of equipment for my journey through life. I realise now that he revelled in Shakespeare, judging by the quantity of commentaries he amassed. He adored Conrad, had a shelf of him and all the books of adventure at sea. He did not garden or golf or play tennis. Reading was his sport. He read and went for long walks.

It fell to my mother to read to us, and what she read laid down the earliest of the patterns, or layers, which shaped my feeling for language: her sense of adventure, travel, and drama; her wish to be *off and doing,* as she put it; and her affinity for Robert Louis Stevenson.

When she read his poems, like "Windy Nights," what patterns was she laying down, what expectations of language and life? What was the nature of the material, heard and reheard, that would load subsequent rehearings—even fifty years later—with so much meaning?

Obviously, the drama of the story: a boy lying awake on a dark and windy night. Does he dream it? Is he really awake? Does the insistent, repetitive mood come from one of those half dreams of the anxious mind hovering between sleep and wake? I often had a dream like that: a doorknob catching a chink of light on the other side of the room would grow enormous and advance at me menacingly, then retreat suddenly, growing infinitely small, only to rush back again, monstrously larger.

The mildly nightmarish quality is heightened by the boy's fretful question, *Why does he gallop and gallop about?* and by the reiterated, emphatic *By, on the highway* . . . *By at the gallop* . . . *By at the gallop* . . . *By he comes* . . . , each of the strong syllables growing in dramatic emphasis by repetition.

I was sick often enough myself and knew from the other

poems that Stevenson was frequently ill, so I knew the sickly boy, tossing in bed, moving a fevered face to find a cool spot on the pillow; his bed clothes snarled from too much turning, adding to the irritation.

That level of the poem provided plenty of nourishment for the melodramatic imagination and self-identification. On another level, not so fearful, it was romantic and exciting. There is the moody scene setting, a gothic night when only those desperate or up to no good would be about and the faint hearted would be glad of their beds.

There is the meter that describes what so tantalizes the listening boy, the galloping rhythm created by the poetic foot (the dactyl) of three syllables—one stressed, two unstressed—as in *by he comes*. Reading it aloud or drumming your fingers in time to the syllables produces an unmistakeable impression of galloping. But that is not all. Stevenson chooses words that sound like the thing he describes, they are onomatopoeic. The *shishing* and *hissing* sounds of *and ships are tossed at sea* is one example. More obvious are the sounds describing the noise of the horse's hooves, the insistent use of the word *gallop,* itself onomatopoeic.

Thus, from this one poem, repeated enough, my mind would be prepared to be receptive to strong active rhythms, descriptive vocabulary, and a vivid, mysterious tale.

Repeated it certainly was. My mother read it as often as we went through *A Child's Garden of Verses,* picking our favourites. But "Windy Nights" was a particular favourite of her mother, my grandmother Daisy Oxner. She took me for walks and made me recite it with her over and over again. She was a Southern belle transplanted to colder climes and she had written a little verse herself, some published by the newspaper in Chattanooga. She had a dramatic way of rendering "Windy

Nights." As we took compulsory walks in the Halifax Public Gardens, she would bounce through it, hitting the stressed syllables with explosive emphasis and riding the meter like a posting horsewoman. When she said the spooky opening line, *Whenever the moon and stars are set,* her voice took on a ghost-story tone and her eyes would open so wide that the whites showed all around the blue, as though she saw something horrible approaching behind me. I knew it was important: she gave it almost as much emphasis as her inevitable question on any outing: the question that would make her stop anywhere, in the middle of a busy sidewalk, clutch my arm, and say with the most deadly seriousness:

"Have you moved your bowels today?"

"Well, Nana, I—"

"Have you, dear, have you? Let me smell your breath." And if that passed:

"Stick out your tongue."

Since Stevenson merited almost the same attention, I didn't forget "Windy Nights."

Nova Scotia lies one time zone closer to England than most of North America, but in the days of my childhood it was spiritually closer still. Psychologically, the province I grew up in was still in large measure a British colony. Halifax society was conditioned by the presence of generations of well-born, sometimes aristocratic, British officers and showed it. The higher up the social pecking order in that small but cosmopolitan seaport town, the more people identified with England. We looked to England for the real juice of our patriotism, our ideals of dress and manners, codes of honour, military dash, and styles of drill, marmalade and gin, pipe tobacco and tweed. We drew spiritual values from the Church of England and humour from *Punch*. It was natural, therefore, that from that fountainhead of everything wise and wonderful came the books that shaped my imagination. When the magic of words first ensnared me, they were words for the most part written in England and intended for English ears: nursery rhymes, Beatrix Potter, *Winnie-the-Pooh, Peter Pan, The Water Babies,* and *The Wind in the Willows*.

Obviously I must have been steeped in British middle-class idiom. After all, Canadian boys didn't say *Oh, bother!* when something annoyed them, or wear *Wellingtons* or *mackintoshes,* as Christopher Robin did, yet I knew them well. They became as familiar as the rubber boots and raincoats we wore. In spite of all this concentrated exposure to English writing, I didn't pick up and use such expressions. They accumulated in a reserve store, a second vocabulary; my dictionary of vicarious literary experience.

What did consciously affect me was the literary landscape. I was, and remain today, highly susceptible to the physical setting described in books. Starting with the Milne stories, part of me began inhabiting or wishing to be in the places they depicted, both the landscape and the emotional climate.

With a few exceptional moments, my life was unclouded and serene. There was the row over the taxi window. At the age of five I was sitting on the curb throwing stones into the street. A taxi passed and one of my stones broke a window. The taxi stopped, the driver grabbed me and marched me up to the house. My mother reacted so strongly that he began pleading with her, "No, don't beat him. It's all right! It was just an accident."

Nothing like that ever happened to Christopher Robin. Nobody threw sand in his eyes, which happened once to me, followed by an agonizing session of having them flushed out with boric acid. Nobody required him to eat everything on the plate—the liver or the scrambled egg which had long gone cold and clammy—down to the last bite, because of the starving Chinese or my moral character. The emotional climate was irresistible, I suppose, because Christopher Robin seemed to be totally in command of his world, as I manifestly was not of mine. He seemed, from a child's perspective, free from arbitrary orders. He decided when to put on his Wellingtons and when to visit his friends. He seemed to live to please himself as long as he bore the tedium of being polite to his elders.

The backdrop to the serenity of this emotional landscape was a physical world which also drew me strongly. It was something else first experienced in these books. The land in a book is a magic land: the author may tell you that it is ugly and barren, devastated by storms or wars, but it will fascinate me as real landscapes often cannot. The mere fact that they form the setting for a story that draws you in, for characters you identify with, casts an enchantment over that place. So it was with the meadows, the woods, the brooks inhabited by Winnie-the-Pooh, Rabbit, Owl, Kanga, and Tigger.

This was my first experience of being drawn into the spell cast by a storyteller whose words spin gossamer bonds that tie your heart and hopes to him. It was the discovery that words make another place, a place to escape to with your spirit alone. Every child entranced by reading stumbles on that blissful experience sooner or later.

For this Canadian child in the thirties there was something more at work. Somehow the idea was planted in me that the English landscape had a spiritual legitimacy that our Canadian landscape did not, because it was always the English landscape we read about. England was where stories were set, where people had adventures: England became the land of story books for me.

English woods, meadows, lanes, and villages stirred feelings that ours did not, as did the words for features of the English landscape not encountered in Canada: *commons, dells, dingles, downs, moors, fells, tarns, burns,* and *becks*—the words were heavy with the promise of adventure.

That played subtly into other Anglophile influences working on me and I grew up putting a special value on things English. The forces drawing me there were irresistible, like a strong elastic band pulling me to the British Isles.

Lots of Americans feel that. For Canadians of my generation struggling, and often losing the struggle, for a national and psychic identity, England became more real than our own world, because of the books we lived in from childhood. It has taken another generation to throw off the vestiges of that psychic colonialism I grew up with, although there are a few shreds of it still left in the Canadian psyche. The seeds of my personal struggle, my personal strain of the virus, must have been planted by the words of Milne, Stevenson, Dickens, and Barrie.

In the garden of the small apartment house we lived in was a very big tree. One day, filled with visions of hollow trees that people could enter, even live in, I attacked the trunk of this tree. The power of imagination or wishful thinking was so strong that it by-passed any sense of physical reality. I actually believed I could cut rooms inside the tree; or, if I made a little effort, a staircase would magically appear. I would ascend the tree into an enchanted storybook world. Under my puny hatchet, the tree suffered no more than a few nicks and I retired very disappointed. I must have been thinking of Owl's tree with its curved steps in the Hundred Acre Wood

My mother with me, aged three

or the hollow-tree entrances to the home of the Lost Boys in *Peter Pan*.

That book made a strong impression at the age of four or five. *Peter Pan* was the first story that actually frightened me a little, just enough fear to make it pleasurable. The snatching of the Lost Boys by the pirates was a moment I could laugh off only when Captain Hook got it from the crocodile which had swallowed the alarm clock, but it left a shadow of anxiety. As for Peter, I never shared his desire not to grow up. I was less moved by the pathetic need to have his shadow sewn back on than by the hard-to-define attractions I felt for Wendy, who did the sewing.

Wendy jumped into my psyche as though there had been a template for her already cut out: the sister I did not have; a subtle blend of comforting maternalism and other vaguely intuited but desirable feminine attributes.

(No sister, but by now I had a brother, Hugh, almost four years younger. He arrived home just before the Christmas on which we had one of the last trees with real lighted candles on the tips of its branches, as memorable for its warm wax smell as for the sight.)

In *Peter Pan* I do not recall being consciously aware of the language, just the stories and the characters. What surprises me now is to find how facetious Barrie's style is, full of coy nudges and arch asides, which, if I had ever noticed them, were forgotten. Even more surprising is the level of the language:

> Next comes Nibs, the gay and debonair, followed by Slightly, who cuts whistles out of the trees and dances ecstatically to his own tunes.

Debonair and *ecstatically* are not nowadays considered vocabulary for children under ten. But then that is true of many of the books considered appropriate to read to us fifty years ago, and probably even truer fifty years before that.

Certainly, *Robinson Crusoe* and *Gulliver's Travels,* written for adults, make no concessions to twentieth-century children. This is Gulliver's scene setting for the naval attack by Blefuscu on Lilliput:

> . . . upon this notice of an intended invasion, I avoided appearing on that side of the coast, for fear of being discovered by some of the enemy's ships, who had received no intelligence of me, all intercourse between the two empires having been strictly forbidden during the war, upon pain of death, and an embargo laid by our Emperor upon all vessels whatsoever.

What happened when I heard words I did not understand? I may have asked occasionally, but I remember clearly never wanting to interrupt the story. Either I got the drift from the context or ignored the words I did not know until some later time. That is how I find myself dealing with foreign languages: asking for translations of some words, guessing at others, remembering, forgetting, but, in net terms, the word command growing by the day.

Archaic language did not put me off. The stories had such compelling narrative ideas—Crusoe marooned alone, Gulliver in a land of people six inches tall—that I listened past the older words, listened harder. When I was aware of them they gave the stories a pleasant flavour, a little additional mystery, part of the atmosphere, like the illustrations of period costumes and weapons. It did not discourage me that Robin Hood said *methinks* and *sooth*.

"Ah, Little John, methinks care for thine own appetite hath a share in that speech, as well as care for me. But in sooth

I care not to dine alone. I would have a stranger guest, some abbot or bishop or baron, who would pay us for our hospitality. I will not dine till a guest be found, and I leave it to you three to find him."

In the *Just So Stories* and *The Jungle Books,* which we read in the same years, Kipling pushed his language right in front of me; I couldn't ignore it, the exotic Indian words, like *Bandar-log* and *dhak* tree, that seemed to have a taste as well as a sound; the strong names for the characters like Tabaqui the jackal, Nag the cobra, and Rikki-Tikki-Tavi, the mongoose. There were also his rhetorical devices, borrowed from the oral story-tellers, repetitions like *the great grey-green, greasy Limpopo River, all set about with fever trees*. They are funny to a child and they grow hypnotic like magic incantations. The repetitions, the sing-song rhythms, and the exotic vocabulary were so suggestive that I imagined I could smell things like the perfumed smoke from a dung fire or the mysterious odour of sandalwood.

Kipling could make me sense a world totally beyond my experience: the heat, the dust, the smells, the clamour, the cries and noises of men and animals. The dark natural forces, like the snakes, were never sentimentalized but in Kipling's hands became both more menacing and yet more tolerable because you were permitted to know their thoughts, too.

Nag waved to and fro, and then Rikki-Tikki heard him drinking from the biggest water jar that was used to fill the bath. "That is good," said the snake. "Now, when Karait was killed, the big man had a stick. He may have that stick still, but when he comes to bathe in the morning he will not have a stick. I shall wait here till he comes." . . . Nag coiled himself down, coil by coil, round the bulge at the bottom of the water jar, and Rikki-Tikki stayed still as death.

Robinson Crusoe was my first full-blooded adult hero and his story enthralled me. I did not know until I got to college and heard about Defoe's place in the social history of England that what I absorbed so avidly was really an exemplar of right values—a model for the emerging British middle class—God-fearing, devout, honest, hard-working, sober, and obsessively protective of property. Something quite bourgeois in me must have responded, because I felt a deepening satisfaction and security as the poor devil retrieved each useful tool or cask of gunpowder from his wrecked ship.

Crusoe was another fictional character instantly congenial to me. I knew that I could cope with being the lone survivor of such a disaster. Crusoe made his isolation so cosy that I envied his being alone to fend for himself so cheerfully.

All these stories were laying down little lessons in psychology, as well as language, and this material was not being laid down in an empty place. New pieces triggered responses from material that was already there, for example, the pleasure it gave me as Crusoe provisioned his cave.

Laid down is a term with many associations—the keel of a ship to be built; fruits preserved for the winter; wine laid down to age. It is the term they use in sound and videotape editing when one track or sequence has been recorded and others will be added and mixed together.

It must be with words as it is with music. Music heard early in life lays down a rich bed of memories against which you evaluate and absorb music encountered later. Each layer adds to the richness of your musical experience; it ingrains expectations that will govern your taste for future music and perhaps change your feelings about music you already know. Certain harmonic patterns embed themselves in your consciousness and create yearnings for repetition, so that you can relive that pleasurable disturbance of the soul. Gradually, your head becomes an unimaginably large juke box, with instantaneous recall and cross-referencing, far more sophisticated than anything man-made.

It is so with words and word patterns. They accumulate in layers, and as the layers thicken they govern all use and appreciation of language thenceforth. Like music, the patterns of melody, rhythm, and quality of voice become templates against which we judge the sweetness and justness of new patterns and rhythms; and the patterns laid down in our memories create expectations and hungers for fulfillment again. It is the same for the bookish person and for the illiterate. Each has a mind programmed with language—from prayers, hymns, verses, jokes, patriotic texts, proverbs, folk sayings, clichés, stories, movies, radio, and television.

I picture each of those layers of experience and language gradually accumulating and thickening to form a kind of living matrix, nourishing like a placenta, serving as a mini-thesaurus or dictionary of quotations, yet more retrievable and interactive and richer because it is so one's own, steeped in emotional colour and personal associations.

The earliest of those layers must date from the first words a baby hears, and certainly from the time a child can understand connected speech and can be read to.

The years I was read to must have lasted until about 1941, when I was ten, well after I had begun school, because it certainly included books I did not read myself, books well beyond the elementary stuff attempted in the first years at school.

Despite all the reading, to me and gradually by me, books

occupied only a small part of my time. Books were there naturally because both parents regarded them as entertainment and diversion. But from infancy until I began reading heavily for myself, books were an experience for bed time or a stormy day or when I was sick. They were not a duty.

There were disagreeable disciplines in my early life. My parents thought good manners very important. One day in 1936 or so, when they couldn't have had a cent to their names, they both dressed formally and gave me lessons in politeness. I was five and not getting it very swiftly. In retrospect, it sounds a little like Henry Higgins with Eliza in *Pygmalion*.

"Now you're meeting Mrs. Grant. What do you say?"

No answer. Mrs. Grant was my godmother. I saw her often.

"You say, 'How do you do, Mrs. Grant. How are you today?' You say it."

"How do you do, Mrs. Grant, and how are you today?"

"No, don't mumble it; say it very clearly."

"How do you do, Mrs. Grant."

"And how are you today!"

"And how are you today?"

"No. No. No. It is: 'How do you *do*.' And look her in the eye. All right now: again, I'm Mrs. Grant and you are meeting me. What do you say?"

From the looks they exchanged I thought they must have suspected they had engendered a social retard, because I was not a quick study at this stuff. They were quite stern about it, and about shaking hands and looking people in the eye. Stern enough—and I remember the scene clearly—to make me very upset, not seeing the point, wanting to stop but being made to go on.

"No one trusts someone who doesn't look them in the eye. They'll think there is something shifty about you. So look me in the eye and shake hands. No! That's a handshake like a limp fish." That was one of my father's favourite expressions.

Why did they care so much? Because they had little else to cling to just then? Because good manners were their birthright? They could wear that badge of their class through the Depression, when they could not afford others. If I was going to make my way in the world, I had to say *sir* and *how do you do,* look people in the eye, shake hands firmly, and get up whenever a woman entered the room.

If I ever thought I was hard done by, I had only to compare the travails of the boys we encountered in Dickens.

Dickens perfectly suited my mother the reader. She read *A Christmas Carol* at the appropriate season every year, *Great Expectations,* and *Oliver Twist,* but it was *David Copperfield* which made the strongest impression on us both. She may have been reading it for the first time. She was of a sentimental disposition, still young and pretty herself, and the mother of two small sons, so the circumstances of the story touched her closely and seared themselves into my feelings. We both trembled and sighed with the story, and my mother wept copiously.

I have not looked at *David Copperfield* again until now, but I experience the same emotions planted by her reading fifty years ago—the sour dread in my stomach about Murdstone and his sister—as though their cruelty could invade our house and plunge us into as much misery as the Copperfields suffered.

I assume that the programming process was thus also adding a layer of sentiments, literary and stylised versions of feelings generated by human affairs beyond my knowing. They became part of the matrix because they were sentiments heavily coloured and textured by the strong feelings of my mother as she read and by my feelings on noticing hers.

Dickens was the first writer I met who could make a small person laugh and cry, be afraid, feel anger at injustice and pride at loyalty and courage, who could arouse feelings of shame and honour. He spoke directly to what must have been my own childhood fears: of sudden descents, chutes, cataclysms that make security vanish in a second: parents lost or dead, orphanhood, forced separations. He touched responsive chords in me: a fear of homelessness, of being a stranger in a vast indifferent world; a child's timidity in communicating in a world of adults. He aroused my sympathy for children being imposed upon, oppressive even when it is comic, like David's treatment by the gluttonous waiter or the space-hogging passengers on the coach to London. He offered the presence and fear of death, violent injury, and accident; a child's fear of physical harm, beating, torture, cruelty; and the relief of escape through the mind, as Copperfield found in his reading. Dickens dealt, as children do, in quick dissolves from laughter to tears, in characters that are very good or very bad.

He was compensatingly rich in the currency of love, security, snugness. His philosophy suited a child's simple fairness: as Aunt Betsy Trotwood promised David, he would be all right if he was straight with her.

What a discovery for a child that all this comes from words, which don't have to be shelled like walnuts, or paid for at one cent each like candies in the glass display case, but can simply be looked at or read to you.

Dickens's words do not lie passively but arouse themselves and reach out to grab you. His words are a show in themselves; language that is constantly dashing out to change its wardrobe, from motley to funereal, clownish to sober citizen, wordy bore to snarling villain, all masking in the end your heart-wrenching reporter. The author is like a clown, constantly delving into his trunk for a different hat and coat. The language is drab only when characters are drab but elsewhere packed with facetious firecrackers, teeming with metaphor—never merely workaday prose. When David and Traddles are seated at the Waterbrooks' dinner party, they are not merely *placed* or *seated* beside certain ladies but

> billeted into two remote corners: he in the glare of a red velvet lady: I, in the gloom of Hamlet's aunt.

When the words do suddenly turn plain, when the rollicking, kidding, nudging, clowning stops, it is to crush your heart with simplicity, as when Peggotty gently tells Davy how his mother died:

> "Peggotty, my dear," she said then, "put me nearer to you," for she was very weak. "Lay your good arm underneath my neck," she said, "and turn me to you for your face is going far off, and I want it to be near." I put it as she asked and oh Davy! the time had come when my first parting words to you were true—when she was glad to lay her poor head on her stupid cross old Peggotty's arm—and she died like a child that had gone to sleep.

It is now as when those words were first read to me by my mother, and my eyes fill with tears. The sad clown's face is real for an instant; then, with your eyes still blinking back tears, he resumes his diverting mad dash into the wings. I see now that he is as crude as all popular entertainment; as full of energy as popular television today, as overdone at times as the laughtrack in a situation comedy. When introducing Steerforth's servant, Littimer, in two paragraphs Dickens uses the words *respectable* and *respectability* a dozen times.

But it is intoxicating language, spell-binding, and the spells haunt my memory since, very early, they became a way of comparing other, real experiences: Scrooge creeping upstairs in his cold, dark house to eat his thin gruel, Pip first meeting Magwitch on the marshes, Copperfield first noticing Uriah Heep:

> it made me uncomfortable to observe that every now and then, his sleepless eyes would come below the writing, like two red suns, and stealthily stare at me for I dare say a whole minute at a time, during which his pen went, or pretended to go, as cleverly as ever.

In spooky passages, or on reading phrases like *stealthily stare,* my mother would widen her eyes at me for a second to share the feel of the words.

David Copperfield may have given me my first taste of irony. Some of it is not subtle but quite obvious enough for a child to realise that he suspects, or actually knows, things the characters do not. Dickens lays it on pretty thick, as in Victorian melodrama, to be understood by the simplest member of the audience. But the irony in *David Copperfield* operates on many levels: as David attributes fine motives to Steerforth, whom the reader sees through; characters like the Micawbers, who deceive themselves but not us; characters like Dr. Strong, who are deceived by others with the reader aware; characters like the Murdstones and Uriah Heep, who proclaim motives transparently false to the reader; or, like Peggotty, who endearingly profess faults they do not possess.

Did I get my taste for melodrama, for satire, for atmospheric mood-writing from Dickens, too? He is where I first encountered them in such vivid colors. Take the satirical introduction of Miss Murdstone:

> and a gloomy-looking lady she was, dark, like her brother, whom she greatly resembled in face and voice; and with very

heavy eyebrows, nearly meeting over her large nose, as if, being disabled by the wrongs of her sex from wearing whiskers, she had carried them to that account. She brought with her two uncompromising hard black boxes, with her initials on the lids in hard brass nails. When she paid the coachman she took her money out of a hard steel purse, and she kept the purse in a very jail of a bag which hung upon her arm by a heavy chain, and shut up like a bite. I had never, at that time, seen such a metallic lady altogether as Miss Murdstone was.

He also gave me, I now realise, the first taste of naturalistic dialogue different from the speech of the rather precocious English children and their middle-class parents encountered in Christopher Robin and Peter Pan.

Reading *David Copperfield* now, I cannot pretend that it is as dark and frightening as it was to my childish ears, and the tone is often facetious in a manner that escaped me then. But Dickens communicated on levels that a very young boy could understand. It is deeply intriguing to me to discover, on making their acquaintance again now, that not only are the characters old friends but the feelings I have about them are, on one level, the feelings I had at the age of eight or ten.

In 1934 the Canadian neurosurgeon Wilder Penfield discovered that if a probe carrying a small electric current touched certain spots in the brain, a patient would experience total recall of a forgotten moment, with sight, sound, smell, whole conversations, and the attendant emotions, all relived. I feel that way about some passages in Dickens: the words and the images they create are indelible and, when reread, act like electrified probes.

David Copperfield triggers such memories. My imagination set the early parts of the book—the arrival of Murdstone, the

Myself in Ottawa, 1939, aged eight

scoldings, the beating—in the small, charming house we moved to in the spring of 1938, when I was seven.

It was the house of my parents' longings after years of moving from apartment to apartment, their place of sweet contentedness. It was a stucco cottage, arched over by tall oak trees on a corner at the end of Oakland Road. It felt like a country house, with a large garden enclosed by hedges and fences, the air coloured and sweetened by flowers and shrubs, the house shaded on hot days by the huge trees. Around the front door was a trellised arbor for roses.

It was a short walk down to the Northwest Arm, an inlet of the sea where for ten cents a ferryman would row you across to the far shore to wooded paths and lakes where we skated and picnicked.

They moved with the help of some sailors from Dad's ship and painted the house themselves. It was an enchanted time for my parents and for us. My father was often home from sea. My mother loved the green things that surrounded the house. We got our first dog. In those dying months of peacetime, the cereal packages contained wonderful models of ocean liners to punch out and assemble. Hugh and I collected piles of acorns that fall and had blistering fights in the evenings with my mother's brother, Breck; hurling acorns at each other across the lawn in the dying light, with the smells of autumn twilight descending on the garden: the scent of cold on the leaves and the burning of piles of leaves from other gardens.

That life was filled with impermanence. We lived there only nine months, because my father was posted to RCMP headquarters in Ottawa and we had to leave the cottage. In the family lore it was regretted ever afterward. That sense of loss and nostalgia and pain I later connected with the reading of *David Copperfield,* when David's house is invaded by the sadistic Murdstones, who force him out of his little paradise. The name *Murdstone* takes some of its cold horror from those feelings and it still rings in my ears with dread. I assume that is what caused my mother to shed such tears over the story. She cried over having lost her beloved house, because, only a few months later, with the outbreak of war, we were back in Halifax and for all the war years lived in an apartment.

"I was a fool to give it up," she said, "but your father is so impulsive. It's always 'up stakes and off we go.'" *Up stakes* was her expression for the rootlessness of my father, which made her anxious. He could abandon any place without a pang, like leaving a campsite and moving on. *Up stakes* was the right image for him; but her stakes instantly grew roots, and they were painful to pull up.

During the war we often passed Oakland Road going to the ferry to cross the Arm. She said, "I was a fool to give it up." I always thought of David Copperfield and his mother, who, in my imagination, had died there.

CHAPTER TWO

The city of Halifax was invented suddenly out of a hillside of birch and balsam fir in 1749 to serve one of the greatest natural harbours of the world—deep, ice-free, and easily defended. It was an aggressive gesture, establishing a base to challenge Louisburg, the mighty French fortress one day's sail to the northeast, and to calm the furious New Englanders. In 1745, they had captured Louisburg in the first great American feat of arms, only to see it given back to France in the Treaty of Aix-la-Chapelle three years later.

Born as a garrison, Halifax thereafter prospered in war and survived the lulls of peacetime. In 1758, the first elected assembly in British North America met in Halifax. Nova Scotia sent four delegates to the Continental Congress in Philadelphia, but the huge British military presence in Halifax kept them neutral and the colony became a refuge for thirty-five thousand Loyalists displaced by the Revolution.

Nova Scotians built swift and graceful ships that traded across the oceans of the world. By 1850, with her fellow maritime provinces, New Brunswick and Prince Edward Island, Nova Scotia accounted for the fourth-largest shipping tonnage in the world. Joshua Slocum, the first person ever to sail around the world for pleasure, alone, was a Nova Scotian, although he sailed from the *Boston States,* as many Nova Scotians called the U.S.

I grew up a *bluenose,* as Nova Scotians are known, supposedly after the color of potatoes grown there. We were always near the sea, familiar with all its sounds—the thunder of coastal surf on granite rocks, the hiss of foam as it runs down a flat beach, millions of bubbles audibly dissolving, and the pores in the sand reopening with tiny snicking sounds. I knew the moan of a foghorn and the clank of a bellbuoy in the fog, the horns of big ships with notes so low they shook your chest, or the *verrup-verrup-verrup* of a destroyer's siren in wartime.

Halifax could be mean, its spartan frame and shingle houses frowning uninvitingly into the sleet-laden winds off the Atlantic; the strong smell of fish blown like a Presbyterian reproach around the frozen corners of the few grand buildings on Barrington and Hollis streets. The shops were provincial, the hotels ungrand, the restaurants unsophisticated. Yet the town had much grace. From behind their lace curtains in the elegant gingerbread houses of the South End, from their comfortable mansions on the Northwest Arm, from their clubs and yachts and mess dinners, well-to-do Haligonians smiled with the assurance of prosperity and culture.

My grandfather Dr. Oxner epitomised the pleasant life the city could offer. He came from Chester Basin on the south shore, a descendant of one of the German families that settled there in the eighteenth century. Returning from Johns Hopkins in Baltimore with his dental degree and his Southern bride, Daisy Neely, he created a civilised life, with a substantial house, bridge and supper parties, golf at Ashburn, teas at the Saraguay Club on the Northwest Arm, lunch at the Halifax Club. He was a dry-fly trout fisherman and escaped annually to the lakes at Kejimkujik.

They entertained and travelled, Daisy often to Europe, and they sent my mother to school in Switzerland when they feared she was getting TB. My grandfather was an erect and dignified figure (he called it *figger*) with a pince-nez perched on a big nose broken when he raced penny-farthing bicycles as a young man (he called them *bye-cycles*). He was a popular man, who walked everywhere with a cane that he swung rhythmically, doffing his hat elaborately to people he knew.

My mother said she knew him angry only once. He was a ceremonial Presbyterian, but in fact non-religious. One day a patient told him she had just seen Peggy going into the convent up Spring Garden Road, wearing a veil and carrying a candle. Dr. Oxner dropped his instruments, left the patient in the dental chair, and ran up the street, past the statue of Robert Burns, to the convent.

My mother loved to tell the story: "He dashed into the chapel, where I was standing in line with the other girls preparing for our First Communion. He was still wearing his dentist's white jacket. He ran up the aisle, grabbed my hand, and pulled me out of there, with my veil and the lighted candle in my hand. He marched me straight home without saying a word, but he told Mother to change my school immediately."

She changed to Halifax Ladies College and was there on December 6, 1917, when the biggest man-made explosion before Hiroshima devastated the north end of the city. An ammunition ship had collided with another and the blast killed nearly two thousand people. All the windows in her school miles away were blown in, as was their front door on Spring Garden Road. In the heavy snowstorm that followed the explosion that night, Dr. Oxner was one of those who got out a horse and sleigh to carry blankets and food to the thousands left homeless.

The Second World War gave Halifax new life. The deep

harbour was crucial in the battle to keep open the North Atlantic lifeline to Britain. Trains from across Canada ground in to the ocean terminals with troops, wheat, munitions, ambulances for the London Blitz, and Bundles for Britain of clothing and food to be loaded into transport ships. More than seventeen thousand ships sailed in convoys assembled or regrouped in Halifax. There they collected the escorts of Canadian corvettes and destroyers to brave the three thousand miles of North Atlantic thick with German submarines.

Back into the harbour, through the submarine net, limped the rusting, battered warships and freighters, their steel hulls crumpled by giant waves or rent by high explosives. More than seven thousand such war-damaged ships needed repairs in Halifax yards. In winter they came in with superstructures swollen with ice from frozen spray; their haggard, chilled crews desperate for land, warmth, food, drink, and women, before they headed back into that hellish sea.

Many ships that left Halifax did not come back. The deep sea bed between Cape Breton Island and Ireland is thick with the shattered metal of their remains. Those who came back brought harrowing, thrilling tales of heroism and terror: of survivors dragged, half-frozen, half-drowned, from the icy waters, or covered in the mucous slime of oil from the tanks of torpoeded ships, or terrible with burns when that oil was ignited and the sea burned.

Yet they went back again and again: in converted liners called AMCs, or Armed Merchant Cruisers, whose tiny guns left them sitting ducks for the U-boat wolf packs; to wallowing tankers, whose cargoes of oil, vital to fuel Britain's war effort, meant certain death if the ship were hit; to the cramped mess decks of corvettes and World War I destroyers, which rolled mercilessly in the long swells, causing a swill of sea water, clothing,

Hugh and I, my mother and father,
on his first wartime leave, 1940

food, and seasick vomit to wash back and forth at their feet with each surge of the sea. They went back to sudden explosions on dark winter nights, and the prospect of jumping for their lives into a black sea so cold it could kill in minutes; to hours on watch, frozen, mittened hands on guns, where no clothing could keep the body warm, as eyebrows and beards caked up with ice. Some were torpedoed many times. But they went back, and their courage matched anything in that war.

My father endured it for the entire war, five and a half years, on gin and cigarettes and the adrenaline of danger, emerging a hero personally decorated by King George, and with a serious heart condition. His comings and goings, the arrivals and departures of the five ships he commanded, punctuated our lives.

The awful reality was partly hidden from us. His visits were exciting because he brought toys from England and chocolate, and because it made my mother so happy. When we were small boys, the worst experiences he ever mentioned were going without sleep and shaving in cold water.

Once when he was home on a quick leave, I went into their bedroom and surprised him half-dressed. He was naked above the waist and his chest was almost covered with wide adhesive tape. My mother shooed me out of the room. They did not want me to see. When he went back to sea, my constant prying forced her to admit that he had been wounded, perhaps by some light shrapnel, or had suffered broken ribs. She wouldn't be precise. It was odd. They were ashamed that we should know he had been hurt. There were no heroics in front of us, as if they did not want the war to be real to us. And yet it was all around us. Our lives were filled with the war.

The streets, shops, restaurants, and rooming houses of the little city swarmed with the uniformed men of many navies, and the anchorages and docks of the harbour were crammed with warships and merchant vessels. German submarines were sinking ships in the approaches to Halifax Harbour. All of our fathers were away at war, mostly in the Navy. The fathers of two of my friends were killed.

There were frequent air-raid alerts, day and night. From our classrooms at Tower Road School, we watched them build a tall platform for an anti-aircraft gun next door. When the sirens wailed, classes stopped as men in steel helmets raced up the steps of the wooden tower to man the gun.

I was a Cub and already impatient to move up to the Scouts, when I discovered that another boy, a year older, had a steel helmet and went out at night on air-raid patrols. I was overcome with envy. The steel helmet did it. I can see it now, hanging over his bedpost, and remember the nonchalant way he devastated me with the information that he was part of the war effort—not a game: the real thing.

"Jeez! They *give* you that helmet?"

"Sure, and a gas mask."

"Holy moly! Let's see! What do you have to do?"

"Well, first you have to be a Scout and you have to be twelve."

"Can I try on the helmet for a minute?"

I had to get into the Scouts, and managed it a few months before my twelfth birthday. That made me eligible to join the Halifax Civilian Emergency Corps. Two evenings a week, they gave me an extensive St. John's Ambulance first-aid course. I became a First-Aid Messenger and was issued a real steel helmet, a gas mask, and a white HCEC arm band. My job, if there was an actual air raid, would be to carry messages between first-aid posts.

There was an air-raid siren on the corner of South Park and Inglis streets, half a block from our apartment. When it went off at night, it sounded loud enough to be right in the bedroom.

I got up and dressed, and put on my gear to report to my post at Pine Hill Divinity School, about a mile away. That meant riding my bike through unlighted streets. None of my close friends' mothers would let them do it, but my mother impressed me by saying I could.

The biggest worry I had was to keep my tyres from slipping into the tram tracks in the dark and to keep my overlarge helmet from falling off when the bike wobbled. Usually I would hang it over the handlebars and put it on just when I went in to report.

At first the adults conscientiously organised mock drills. People playing wounded were brought in to be bandaged and splinted up, and I dashed off to take messages because the phones were supposed to be out. Mostly we sat around the post drinking cocoa, trying to stay awake until the all clear, then went home to bed.

It was exciting being out at night, all by myself, on my bike in the dark—not the boy inside listening, half-afraid, but the man outside, galloping by on an adventure.

I developed complicated feelings about Germans, the people my father was out there fighting. He told us the U-boat crews were honourable, for the most part, not like the Nazis, but fine sailors in a fine naval tradition. Of course, he said, there were occasional Nazi *scum* among them; that accounted for stories of crews of torpedoed ships being machine-gunned in the water.

My mother told us many times that her father, Dr. Oxner, came from "nice Germans—peace-loving people from Hanover, not Prussians."

But the Germans were also a joke: on one of Dad's ships the crew rigged up a loud-speaker system on deck. If his depth charges ever forced a U-boat to the surface, he intended to bombard them with Spike Jones and the City Slickers playing

"Right in der Führer's Face." That was very popular on the radio and very funny to small boys—rude raspberry sounds syncopated with the band in the chorus:

> Vee go Heil! (*Pbsspbt!!*)
> Heil! (*Pbsspbt!!*)
> Right in der Führer's face.

To let us enjoy the effect, they rehearsed when Hugh and I visited the ship. The same system played "McNamara's Band" full blast when the ship entered Londonderry or Belfast at the end of a convoy.

The Germans we saw in the highly propagandistic movies of the war years were scary but not very real. They were sadistic and bad-tempered and they always lost. But they provided essential vocabulary for our endless war games. We chose who played Germans the way we eliminated for any game, as English-speaking children have for hundreds of years, with little variations: *Eeny, meeny, miney, mo* or *One potato, two potato, etc*.

Those eliminated had to be Germans, meaning they had to die obediently when machine-gunned with appropriate *eh-eh-eh-eh-eh* or *tchooo* noises, but they had the compensation of being able to shout *Achtung* and *Schweinhund* liberally.

What convinced me that Germans were real people, human beings, was inspecting a captured Messerschmitt ME-109 fighter. It was on show for some fund-raising purpose and I waited in line to pay ten cents for a few moments inside the cockpit. Sitting in the pilot's seat, not large even for a boy, gave me an eerie feeling. The spartan, utilitarian grey metal interior, the places where the German pilot's feet and hands had worn the metal shiny, putting my thumb on the button that fired the wing-mounted machine guns made me think I could almost smell the person who had sat there when the plane was forced down in England. The few instruments had German labels and the realisation that the man who flew this had to be able to read the words which I could not made him intelligent, alive—a real person with a name. So were the Germans who had designed and built this beautiful machine, even if it was *no match for our Spitfires, of course*. I got out and went home feeling I had had an important experience.

Through the Scouts we took part in a lot of salvage drives, going around in big trucks collecting paper or aluminum pots and pans. One Saturday the object was paper and the collection point was our school on Tower Road. In one attic we found a pile of *Esquire* magazines, and although we were decidedly prepubertal, the very word *Esquire* had a naughty, exciting connotation. *Esquire* meant *Varga girls*—the nearest thing to suggestive pictures I saw during my childhood. We hid the *Esquire*s in a corner of the truck and, when we got to the school, left them till last. Finally, we each put several of the heavy magazines under our sweaters, picked up stacks of innocent publications, and marched into the school. When we came out again, the principal, Mr. Seamans, was standing by the front door, inspecting the traffic. He spotted the contraband shapes under our sweaters and made us reveal them. He was shocked, or pretended to be; outraged at such depravity. He marched us up to his office and gave us each six wallops with the strap on our hands. Strapping was a common occurrence for us in the classrooms, but administered by a heavyset man instead of a lady teacher, it was a sobering experience. Western civilisation was falling apart, but in Halifax our morals were being guarded.

Even with all this swirling about the small city, the South End of Halifax offered us a very sheltered childhood. It was tame in terms of sensations, and real life could seldom duplicate the calamities we encountered in books.

When we heard that a woman had jumped from the Young Avenue Bridge and been run over by a train, we raced down there on our bikes but were disappointed to find they had already shovelled sand over the blood. When a distraught American naval officer murdered his wife and daughters with an axe and fled into the woods across the Arm, we went to the gates of the house to drink in the atmosphere of horror. We prowled the ruins of an abandoned prison in Franklin Park, convinced that what we smelled was the bones of prisoners hanged and buried inside the walls. We played in the eighteenth-century Martello tower in Point Pleasant Park, relishing the opening where boiling pitch had been hurled down on attacking Indians.

Our geographical frame was very small. We shared the fear of the ancient navigators about the unknown, and we marked parts of our psychological maps of the city with dangers we only guessed at. Only a few blocks down Inglis Street the docks began. It would have taken three minutes to go there on our bikes, but we did not. For years the street names, Water, Granville, Hollis, and stretches of Barrington suggested danger and vice and we stayed away, while finding our own ways of getting into trouble.

All the fruit trees in the fenced gardens of the neighbourhood we considered fair game if we could raid them without getting caught. We approached shoplifting in the same spirit.

John Godfrey, son of another naval officer, and I haunted the five-and-ten on Barrington Street for months, picking up a flashlight, crayons, pencils, erasers, marbles. We called it *swiping,* not *stealing.* The technique was to stroll along the counters, picking up and examining many things and carefully putting them back. The salesgirls continued to see two boys handling things but always returning them. We must have turned careless the afternoon we targeted a date stamp and ink pad. Godfrey had the ink pad and I had the stamp with rotating dates when we said:

"Well, I guess it's time to go home."

"Yes, my mother will be wondering where I am."

I had started out one door and he the other, when I got stopped by a big man who grabbed my arm and said, "Come back inside, young man. The manager wants to see you."

I was terrified. So was Godfrey. I saw his white face a few yards away at the curb. I was marched to the rear of the store and into a little office.

The manager made me empty my pockets, then asked for my telephone number. I gave it: 3-4610. He called my mother, and I could hear her exploding with such wrath at the other end that he ended up saying to her, "Yes, I'll send him home right now. But don't be too hard on him. He's had a good lesson. I don't think he'll do it again."

He hung up and said to me, "Your mother says you're to go straight home and *she'll* deal with you. And if I catch you at it again, I'll send for the police next time."

Outside, I found Godfrey. "Do they know about me?" he asked.

"I don't think so."

"What did they do?"

"They called my mother."

"Golly, do you think she'll tell mine?"

We went home, slowly, walking, not taking the tram, to give my mother time to calm down. We didn't talk much.

"Are you scared?" he asked me.

"Sure. Are you?"

"Only if your mother tells my mother. She'll kill me."

"I think my mother is going to kill *me*."

She was still in a rage when I climbed the stairs to the second-floor apartment and opened the door. She did not take the store manager's advice.

"I've never been so ashamed. All the years I've lived in this city—and your grandparents—nothing ever happened like this. Go into the bathroom!"

The bathroom was the punishment room. On the rare occasions my father spanked Hugh or me, he did it there.

"I'm glad your father isn't here. He would die of shame to think that a son of his would be stealing. How hard he's worked to give you everything you could want, and now, just because he's away at sea for months at a time—" and she dissolved into tears. "Take off your pants!"

"The man in the store said not to be too hard on me!"

"Never mind the man in the store! You're lucky not to be in jail. Bend over the bathtub!"

I bent over the tall old-fashioned bathtub with ornate feet. She had a heavy wooden hairbrush and brought it down with all her might on my bare backside about eight times. It really hurt. She was weeping and shouting.

"Don't you ever (*whack*) ever (*whack*) let me hear of you doing such a thing again. Now go to your room. You'll have no supper and you'll have lots of time to think this over."

It was like the scene where Murdstone beat David Copperfield, except that I felt no resentment, believing the punishment quite just. I was still gripped by the enormity of having been caught and relief at escaping so lightly.

We also used to raid the soft-drink truck that stopped on South Street behind Drew King's house on Kent Street. Every

Saturday morning the truck would park in front of a house across the street. We believed that the driver had a lady friend, because he never delivered any bottles there. Four of us—Drew King, Harold Stevens, Norman Smith, and I—would lie in wait behind the tall wooden gate, eyes level with the top. We pretended it was a German supply truck. As soon as he disappeared, one of us would vault over the gate—commando-style, learned from the movies—rush to the truck, grab the first quart-size bottle of pop he could reach, and race back. The others opened the gate a crack and we all ran down the long garden to the old stables to open the bottle with a jackknife. Sometimes we liberated pop nobody liked, like cream soda, but it didn't matter much: the bottle was so shaken up by its hectic journey that we lost half the drink in spray.

We had done that one Saturday morning in early fall 1941, when the others began teasing me that my mother was going to have a baby, as though her very obvious pregnancy should embarrass me. It did. I wanted to drop the subject but couldn't, because they all persisted and because they had such absurd notions of how a baby was born. They really wanted information. One suggested that a baby came into the world through the rectum, a theory the others began to discuss. It quickly degenerated into little boys' bawdiness, with a lot of delighted, if uneasy, laughter. Someone suggested that at the hospital, to help the baby out, a woman would be given an enema and the doctor would hold a sieve to catch the baby so that it was not flushed down the toilet. That very practical suggestion produced hysterical laughter. I protested, both to defend my mother from the undignified suggestions and also because it suddenly dawned on me that I actually knew the big truth: women had another orifice.

Several months earlier, a casual friend, Charlie Bains, had

pestered me to come home to look at his mother's copy of *Gray's Anatomy,* which he had just discovered. His mother was a nurse. The visit had to be put off several times to make sure she was going to be out. Eventually, with much stealthy opening and shutting of doors in the empty house, he unveiled the fat book and showed me what he called the "juiciest bits."

What made a profound impression on me was a graphic illustration of childbirth at the moment of crowning. One glimpse banished ignorance, and innocence, forever. Until then I had not known the vagina existed. To discover that it did and in the same moment see it stretched so unbelievably to pass the baby's head made me feel sick. I went home wishing I had never looked at the book, vowing never to pry into such mysteries again. I felt guilty and unclean, knowing something I was not meant to know.

Some of the dread must have lingered, because I repressed the knowledge until that Saturday morning. I told the other boys, but they didn't believe me, *Gray's Anatomy* or not. If the four of us had been voting on the question that morning, the meeting would have decided by a 3–1 majority that babies are born anally, because that is the only possible opening.

We were Anglicans, my mother fervently, my father ceremoniously, and the Cathedral of All Saints on Tower Road was one of the hubs of my young life. The Church of England did not provide me with any spiritual awakening, nor any intimacy with God, but it anointed me with language; yea, verily, it steeped me in it. We attended once every Sunday until I joined the choir, and then it was twice, occasionally three times, not to mention choir practice one evening a week.

All Saints was not a rich church. Its front was unfinished for lack of funds, the omission masked for many years by a grey wooden façade. The simple Gothic interior was stained by many water leaks from ill-fitting leaded windows. These chalky streaks gave the stuccoed walls and the carved stone columns a patina of false antiquity. Otherwise it was very plain, with little ornamentation, because too few generations of Haligonians had passed on to be commemorated and too few sinners had cluttered the place with benefactions in hope of purchasing redemption.

That also meant that the cathedral was unusually bright, because it could not afford stained glass in the windows of the transept. They carried a substitute glazing with a faint green or pink cast, suggesting reverence-in-waiting. That admitted lots of God's sunshine, and especially on bright winter days with light reflected from the snow, the whole cathedral flushed out the shadowy spirituality of the Old World with the honest clarity of the New.

Until, as a member of the choir, I became an actor in the drama I loathed going to church. The service seemed endless and meaningless; I never knew why or where it was going. My knees ached from the hard prayer benches. And I hated, on a non-school day, having to put on suit, collar, and tie and shine my black shoes. Several times I solved the problem by fainting and forcing my mother to leave.

I could sense it coming on. The air would become thick and unbreathable; the space in front of my eyes would dissolve into a grey-green mist that turned objects increasingly fuzzy. My stomach would feel as if I were about to be sick and—then— I would be crumpling up on the floor, causing a stir, being fanned and helped outside. Once out in the fresh air, I instantly recovered. Like Tom Sawyer's Aunt Polly, my mother thought I was faking, but I wasn't, and it happened often enough that

I could use it as a threat. "If you make me go to church today, I'll faint! You know I will." Occasionally it worked.

All Saints was not, to my mother's regret, High Church enough to burn incense, but it had a mélange of smells that became the odour of sanctity for me. The chancel was perfumed with beeswax candles and strongly scented flowers. There was the smell of the varnish of the pew backs against which I pressed my face while pretending to pray; the starched smell of the freshly laundered surplices of ministers and choir against the mustier odour of the less often cleaned cassocks; and the bouquet of many soaps and scents of worshippers newly bathed for their devotions.

There was also a waft of stale body odour noticeable when the School for the Blind occupied the usual block of seats in the nave. Their smell of neglect, their chopped hair and motley clothing repelled yet saddened me, reminding me of my clean home and the Sunday roast then cooking. They were what I imagined the inmates of David Copperfield's school or the workhouse in *Oliver Twist* to be like: kept by the principle that creatures deprived in one sense wouldn't notice deprivation in most others. Since these blind youngsters couldn't notice what they looked like, the institution didn't. They sat at the front of the church, touching each other to know when to rise or kneel. They were like medieval carvings, holding their heads at awkward angles and making strange grimaces as they lifted clouded eyes towards the beams of light from the transept windows. They compelled me to stare and to be ashamed of staring at their misfortune.

If there was an odour of sanctity, there was also its sound. Forced attendance meant that I was compelled for years to listen to and to utter some of the most glorious prose in the language. In print it meant nothing to me at first, and I'm not sure that it meant anything aurally for a long time, but the words, spoken, chanted, or sung, resonant and important, sank in.

The diction of the Anglican Church in Canada in those days was crisply English, with vowels arched to reverberate in Gothic spaces and consonants bitten out so that they clicked back from the stone walls. It was highly theatrical speech, a professional voice like that adopted by Shakespearean actors in Canada and the United States. The rounded tones lost clarity but gained drama in the confused acoustics of All Saints, further scrambled by a weak amplification system.

There was poured into the porches of this child's mind a rich, echoing soup of sound which made literal sense only when recollected years later. If scientists could examine my brain, as they do the contents of murder victims' stomachs, they would find that I had gorged myself when young on plum puddings and fruitcakes of this seventeenth-century prose; each word simple in itself, the combination rich and fruity, loved for the taste on the tongue, though years in the digesting; words for their own sake. That was particularly true of the often-repeated passages from the Book of Common Prayer, paraphrases of biblical verses that constitute English worship since the sixteenth century.

> Lighten our darkness, we beseech thee, O Lord; and by thy great mercy defend us from all perils and dangers of this night.
>
> The Lord bless thee, and keep thee.
> The Lord make his face shine upon thee and be gracious unto thee:
> The Lord lift up his countenance upon thee, and give thee peace.

Let the words of my mouth, and the meditation of my heart, be acceptable in thy sight, O Lord, my strength and my redeemer.

Forgive us our trespasses as we forgive those who trespass against us. And lead us not into temptation, but deliver us from evil: For thine is the kingdom, and the power, and the glory, for ever and ever. Amen.

Incantations absently said hundreds of times in hundreds of moods, the needle playing the same groove again and again until the phrases have a hypnotic, even narcotic effect, independent of meaning.

Those were the early words, which I said and sang as a member of the cathedral choir. I took great pleasure in the singing. It was fun when there were settings with descants, as at Christmas and Easter, with the entire congregation as well as the choir singing and the great organ thundering away, to come in over the top of it all with our treble voices hitting the highest notes.

There were moments when the thrill was greater. During the processional hymns, when the choir paraded around the whole church, it was gratifying to hear our loud, trained voices alongside the puny efforts of the ordinary members of the congregation. If one of them—insufficiently awed—presumed to compete with us, we sang even louder, to drown the upstart out. On one of those occasions, I heard a woman say to another as the boys' section of the choir passed by, "Aren't they sweet!" We did not feel "sweet." We felt powerful and important. But she made me realise the theatrical effect we were having: our twelve-year-old scruffiness hidden under newly-starched ruffs and surplices, our hair clean and combed, beams of light from the high windows of the nave striking us picturesquely, as our clear voices soared out vigorously—more or less in tune.

Vanity of vanities, saith the preacher, all is vanity. Perhaps that is why the adults in the choir kept coming back year after year, and put up with our snickering, our telling dirty jokes behind our music sheets, as we hunched down in the choir stalls laughing at some big-bosomed lady of the choir; our parking gum behind the carved angels or rattling marbles in our pockets; our not knowing the place, or missing our cue, or singing off tune, or being late for practice. We boys got paid ten cents a service, triple during festivals. The adults got nothing.

Before my voice changed, it grew sure enough to carry a little solo work with school choirs, which terrified me but added to the gratification.

None of this made me religious, but it had the side effect of making me much more conscious of the sound of words. Disciplined singing demanded not only musical training but exercise in diction. Singing the phrase *Lord, now lettest thou thy servant depart in peace, according to thy word* requires that the words be stretched out to fit the musical setting. You cannot expand a word like *peace,* as rock singers do now, by splintering it into many syllables, *pee-ee-ee-ees,* with a little grunt of air on each. You have to ride the one syllable smoothly and elastically for a bar or more of the music.

I came to understand the value of the vowels and wanted, when speaking or reading them, not singing, to give them full measure. It was the same with the consonants in singing. If the piece was a quiet setting for a psalm, we learned to give the terminal *d*'s and *t*'s enough notice with our tongue and teeth so they would carry, without at the same time exaggerating them.

Also, we became thoroughly familiar with all the anachronistic verb forms, like the second person singular, *When thou doest alms, let not thy left hand know,* and the third person, *what thy right hand doeth*. Such phrases do not come trippingly off the tongue if the mind still trips on them. Repeated use made the idiom perfectly familiar. Twisters for twentieth-century tongues like

> And why beholdest thou the mote that is in thy brother's eye, but considerest not the beam that is in thine own eye?

heard or said often enough become part of the pattern of one's thinking; in effect, another language learned in childhood. Hitting the English poets, from Elizabethans onwards, a few years later, was like parachuting into friendly territory, my basic Berlitz course already memorised. And, as with music, affection grows with familiarity.

All this exposure to the King James Bible, the Book of Common Prayer, and the hymns seasoned me with the words and the forms that had launched British navies and armies into battle and imperial civil servants on their missions; the words that had christened the babies, married the daughters, and buried the dead of the Empire:

> Naked came I out of my mother's womb, and naked shall I return thither: the Lord gave, and the Lord hath taken away; blessed be the name of the Lord

were still being pronounced over my generation of Canadians. It was like the tannin of English tea staining our souls for life. You do not lose it ever.

> Far called, our navies melt away;
> On dune and headland sinks the fire:
> Lo, all our pomp of yesterday
> Is one with Nineveh and Tyre!

> Lord God of hosts, be with us yet
> Lest we forget, lest we forget.

We sang with lusty pride the great hymns of an empire, in the 1940s still largely intact.

> Land of Hope and Glory, Mother of the Free,
> How shall we extol thee, who are born of thee?
> Wider still and wider shall thy bounds be set;
> God, who made thee mighty, make thee mightier yet.

And Blake's thrilling poem, somehow appropriated by muscular, industrial, martial Christianity,

> And did those feet in ancient time
> Walk upon England's mountains green?
> And was the holy Lamb of God
> On England's pleasant pastures seen?
>
> I will not cease from mental fight,
> Nor shall my sword sleep in my hand
> Till we have built Jerusalem
> In England's green and pleasant land.

At the very beginning of the Second World War, in the spring of 1940, all the school children of Halifax, dressed in white, were massed on the Wanderer's Ground. We filled the bleachers and sang in our thousands of little voices the songs of the First World War:

> We're the soldiers of the Queen, my lads . . .
>
> There's a long, long trail a-winding . . .
>
> Keep the home fires burning . . .
>
> It's a long way to Tipperary . . .

And when the songs of the Second World War came along, we sang them with stirring hearts, as though they were hymns:

> There'll always be an England
> And England shall be free . . .
>
> There'll be bluebirds over
> The white cliffs of Dover . . .

The war took on a kind of religious meaning; singing stirring songs about the defence of England was on the same level as singing hymns praising God and praying for victory, except that the songs were more appealing. Gracie Fields singing "wish me luck as you wave me goodbye" moved me so much when played at a friend's summer cottage that I became acutely homesick and had to be sent home.

Every day before classes at Tower Road School we sang a hymn, and it was often

> O, hear us when we cry to Thee
> For those in peril on the sea!

which I sang with burning eyes but full of pride. Psalm 107 had the same effect on me:

> They that go down to the sea in ships,
> That do business in great waters.

The war provided another kind of playground. In calm moments in harbour, we had the run of my father's ships. The crews were anxious to please us, and generous with soda pop, sailors' knives with marlin spikes, cap tallies, bosun's calls, and lanyards. We could climb anywhere on those ships and, through naval friends, on any other British or Canadian ships in port. They included great battleships like the Royal Navy's *Revenge*. When I was on a private tour of *Revenge* one day, a British sailor took me into one of the forward turrets with its 15-inch guns. He opened the breech of one and for a thrill lifted me head and shoulders into the shining brass-and-steel opening, to look up the long barrel with its grooved rifling twisting away almost to infinity.

"Give you a taste of what it feels like to be a shell on its way to Jerry," he said. *Revenge* was later lost in action.

A British merchant service captain gave children's parties in the former luxury liner he now commanded as a troop ship. We children raced shrieking through the ornate dining salons and ballrooms, empty of everything except their gilt ceilings and mirrors and the ghosts of peacetime voyagers.

The smells and sounds of the insides of ships became as familiar as those of the classrooms at school.

It was taken for granted that I was going into the Navy, so I was an eager sponge for naval lore. I knew ships' names, tonnages, armaments, and speeds, as other children knew baseball statistics. When I began reading hungrily for myself, I soaked up my father's collection of naval adventures from World War I, by authors like "Taffrail," with titles like *The Man from Scapa Flow*.

I knew about life at Osborne, the Royal Naval College, and the trials of a midshipman in detail. I fought the Napoleonic Wars at sea vicariously with C. S. Forester's Horatio Hornblower. From Nordhoff and Hall's *Mutiny on the Bounty*, I learned the sadistic rigors of discipline in a press-ganged Navy. I picked up phrases like *All hands lay aft to witness punishment. . . . Bring her up into the wind a little, Mr. Bush, and we'll*

*give Frenchy a whiff of grapeshot . . . Steady as she goes . . .
Beat to quarters . . . Man the t'gallants . . . Avast there, me
hearties . . . hearts of oak,* and so on.

I do not remember actually learning to sail, but by eleven I
could handle a small dinghy. We never had boats of our own,
but sailed other people's whenever we could.

Outside Halifax, Nova Scotia is a sweet and quiet world, full
of soft, cool places. The trees grow down to the sea on the long
fingers of granite embracing hundreds of deep coves and harbours. In the shadows under the trees are cushioned floors of
mosses and ferns. The woods are perfumed with the sweet smell
of balsam firs and the pine needles underfoot.

My grandmother and mother both noticed everything in nature. I learned what you could safely eat, like the spicy tea
berries growing among the mosses and lichens on the granite,
and what you could not, like pigeon berries. We could fill
buckets with wild strawberries from the fields, blueberries from
the rocky ledges, blackberries and raspberries along the stone
walls and fences. We ate Indian pears, choke cherries, and wild
cherries, as well as plums, pears, and apples from cultivated
varieties that had seeded themselves.

My grandmother picked bayberries, and when the leaves
dried and fell off, she put the grey stems with clusters of paler
grey berries in a Chinese vase. She knew the dark places in the
woods for lady's slippers and where to rummage under the dried
grass and leaves of early spring for the heavily-perfumed may-
flowers. My grandfather showed me how to pick dried resin
from the spruce trees to chew as gum, and that you could drink
the pure water collected in Indian cups. Among them they
taught me the names of every kind of wild flower, tree, shrub,

and grass. I liked the precision of that: looking at a tree and knowing at a glance that it is a maple or an oak, not just a tree.

They communicated not only knowledge but joy.

"Look, Rob, look!" my mother would say, about a bud in early spring, a sunset, a maple in the fall, the first evening star, the new moon. "Oh, look, look!" with real excitement and a rush of emotion in her delight for the natural things around her.

Their expressions, more than the words they used, passed on their deep joy and made it mine. When I go out now at the first crack of spring, I cannot resist saying, as they would, "Oh, smell the new earth!" as a man coming out of a cave after a long winter must have remarked twelve thousand years ago.

They made the outdoors congenial, the woods a protective, safe retreat, not hostile or frightening.

Roving the woods and beaches began in the summer of 1942, when my father got a sudden two-week leave to spend with us and the baby, Michael, who had arrived the previous December. The school year was not over, but my mother took us out of school and rented a simple cottage at Hubbards on St. Margaret's Bay. It was still very cold in the mornings and at night, and my father kept large fires of birch logs going. The kitchen had a wood-burning cast-iron range and he showed me how to split kindling and smaller logs for cooking fires. When he went back to sea, I had that chore for the rest of the summer, as well as helping to wash diapers and hang them out to dry, mix formula from milk and Crown Brand corn syrup, and feed it to Michael.

There was plenty of incentive to break away whenever possible to a platform I made high in a pine tree in the woods behind the house, or to roam the vacant beaches, glad to be alone.

Wandering on miles of empty beaches, or in the meadows and forests adjoining them, I had the feeling that every one had left a long time ago and that no one ever came here now. Yet these landscapes were filled, it seemed, with human energy; perhaps the sadness of people who had to leave. As a boy I thought it was the war that had made them leave, not hard times.

Whether that emptiness of beaches and woods conditioned me, or just suited my personality, I don't know. It fitted a boy who liked to wander off to create space and silences for himself. I liked the solitude the summer time made possible.

I had the soul of a beachcomber, content to wander for hours along the shore picking up whatever the sea had brought in, all the flotsam from sunken ships, once a sailor's hat with no tally. I lived with dread for the day when I would find a body washed up, but none obliged my ghoulish fancy.

It seemed that the sea related to everything we did. When they were engaged my father had given Masefield's *Salt Water Ballads* to my mother. She would recite lines from it as she stood by a foggy shore in summer:

> I must down to the seas again, for the call of the running
> tide
> Is a wild call and a clear call that may not be denied;
> And all I ask is a windy day with the white clouds flying,
> And the flung spray and the blown spume, and the
> sea-gulls crying.

I have an image of her on a long, empty beach; walking barefoot a little apart from us, with her own thoughts, stopping to write something with a stick in the sand; then when we run up, erasing it with a girlish smile—half pleasure, half embarrassment.

CHAPTER THREE

I suppose I grew up thinking about the sea as a boy in Kansas or Saskatchewan might think about the land the family farmed.

My family no longer owned any land and how that had come about was a tale of some bitterness to my mother: my father never talked about it. His grandfather William MacNeil built a house in North Hatley, Quebec, and they came north from Lancaster, Massachusetts, to summer there. Dad's father, Robert Ware MacNeil, was raised as a gentleman and could not do much else. The property he inherited slipped through his fingers. It was one of the episodes in my mother's moral history of life.

"He was a fool with money; a charming man, but a fool with money. Let that be a lesson to you. It's the curse of the MacNeils!"

I never met that grandfather. While I was still a small child, he removed his war injuries from the Montreal winters to California. I knew him only from birthday cards bearing an American dollar bill and good wishes in a strong black copperplate.

Because we did not have land, perhaps the sea became a substitute, since it was as much ours as anybody's.

I know it is bad science but the notion continually returns

to me that a feeling for the sea is in my genes. My father was not a professional Scot, the way many North Americans are. He didn't put on Highland dress or learn the bagpipes. But he was stirred by the history of the Clan MacNeil and our presumed origins on the island of Barra in the Western Hebrides.

Parents can plant magic in a child's mind through certain words spoken with some thrilling quality of voice, some uplift of the heart and spirit. They spoke the word *Hebrides* with such a tone of reverence and nostalgia that it took on magical associations for me.

Hebrides has classical echoes traced to the Latin *Hebudes* found in Pliny and the Greek of Ptolemy. Yet appropriately it has a Gaelic softness, suggesting mists and luminous light in tones of pearl grey and heather, with occasional shafts of gold when the sun breaks through the overcast. It suggests above all the sea that surrounds those islands.

We are descended from the Scots Celts and their Norse conquerors. Some genealogists call them the people of the Black Galley, the heraldic representation of a Viking longboat with banked oars and a single sail that descends from Norse and Swedish kings of the seventh century to the family crests of many Scottish clans today, including the MacNeils'. My father took it for his bookplate to express his own love of the sea and our presumed lineage.

But the galley suggests an even mistier heritage, from the seagoing peoples of the eastern Mediterranean. That is what the oral legends say: that the clan started with a man called Niall of Scythia, who was minister to an Egyptian Pharaoh and gave his name to the river Nile.

After separating from the Irish Neils (Neil of the Nine Hostages and all that), the MacNeils who settled in Scotland became a small and rowdy clan, not known for their meekness or modesty. They had nearly a thousand years of storm-bound winter nights in their tiny castle and crude island houses in which to spin fantastic tales of their origins. For those who like such romantic stuff, there is some archaeological evidence that, coming by stages to Spain, Brittany, the Channel Islands, Cornwall, Ireland, Wales, Mediterranean peoples reached the Hebrides as long ago as 2500 B.C. There may be a cultural link in the bagpipes, the Irish-Scots instrument also known to North Africans, Arabs, Turks, Greeks, and the people of the Caucasus.

Whatever the origins of the early Celts, reliable history documents their fusion with the Norse, who ruled the Hebrides from A.D. 888 to 1266. Their mingled bloods created an island people both lyrical and daring, living in hard intimacy with the sea. The sea fed them, defended them, made them fiercely independent, and nourished an incessant wanderlust. Yet when the cruelties of history, or a simple taste for adventure, drove them away over the oceans of the world, the Hebrides remained in their hearts as a constant yearning. There is a song of exile that survives in Nova Scotia:

> From the lone shieling on the misty island,
> Mountains divide us and a waste of seas;
> Yet still the blood is strong, the heart is Highland,
> And we, in dreams, behold the Hebrides.

Not only were they superb and intrepid sailors, but they wove the ocean into their songs and the Gaelic language, which finds at least ten ways to say sea or ocean. So much was the sea a part of their thinking that their names for its moods combine to describe people with sea-like characteristics, thus *aigean* means ocean, while *aigeannach* means high-mettled, self-willed, spirited; and *aigeantach* means a turbulent female. By contrast, *muir* means sea in a sweeter mood, and *muirn* means cheerfulness, joy, delicateness, tenderness, affection; and *mùir-neag* is a cheerful girl, or a delicate, tender woman. To make similar words in English we would have to say something like *sea-raging-woman* or *sea-sweet-girl*. Kenneth MacLeod, a collector of island music, wrote in *Songs of the Hebrides* in 1917:

> The sea has cast her spell upon the impressionable Celt—her generosity, her might, her playfulness, her frequent cruelty are felt, but what really haunts the Celtic mind is her awful mysteriousness.

Another Gaelic word for ocean, *cuan*, forms several adjectives, such as *cuantach*, sea-bred, and *cuanta*, able, robust, and the noun *cuanard*, stormy sea. *Cunard*, of course, is the name of the first regular Atlantic steamship line, started by Sir Samuel Cunard, of Halifax.

Out of the atmosphere of values every family breathes of what is good and what is bad, I knew that the sea was good. I took for granted that it built character to go to sea, to wrest your living from it, to respect it, to be in awe of its terrible powers, but to take it as a matter of course that you went down to it and did business with it. In our mythology, everything to do with the sea was clean and honourable work.

Awareness of the sea used to be far more common than it is today, when air travel has made the oceans seem puny and most people think of boats only for pleasure. Experience of the sea used to be central in the lives of the English-speaking peoples; and knowledge of oceans was vital to commerce, exploration, and conquest.

The sea was so familiar a part of Western life from the Elizabethans to the twentieth century that expressions relating to it became metaphors for activities on the land. Such expressions filled the language I heard or read in the books about the sea that I began devouring at twelve or thirteen.

Everybody depended on *his ship coming in*. They were *all in the same boat*, waiting till *the bitter end*. In everyday life, they would *back and fill*, or be *taken down a peg or two* if they didn't *know the ropes*. They had to keep *a weather eye open* and give a stranger *a wide berth* if he was *bearing down on them* and they didn't like *the cut of his jib*, because he might be *armed to the teeth*, at least until he *showed his true colours* or *nailed his colours to the mast*. If he *spliced the mainbrace* before *the sun was over the yardarm*, put too much *grog on the rocks* and *down the hatch*, got *three sheets to the wind* and *keeled over*, he might have to *trim his sails* and *pour oil on troubled waters* to *get on an even keel*, or risk being *keel-hauled*. If they *slacked off* or *rested on their oars*, *weren't pulling their own weight*, or *sailed too close to the wind*, someone might *lower the boom* and *take the wind out of their sails*, forcing them to *chart a new course*. *In the doldrums*, if they didn't *make headway* and were *dead in the water*, they might be *all at sea* and long for a *safe harbour*, because *time and tide wait for no man*. If *landlubbers shoved off* and ventured on the *high seas*, *come hell or high water*, where it wasn't all *plain sailing*, they'd have to *hit the decks* and *haul it* or be *half seas over* and even *pooped* before they could *drop anchor* or *barge in* to put their *port* side alongside the dock for the *longshoremen* to discharge cargo. If some *tar* listened to too much *scuttlebutt* and talked *a lot of bilge*, they might *give him some leeway* or tell him to *pipe down* or put him in the *booby hatch* if he and the captain were *at loggerheads*. If a ship was *first-rate*, and the captain no *figurehead*, he'd have her *shipshape from stem to stern*, so *by and large* she'd get *a clean bill of health*. Then the *swab* could *clear the decks*, *stow it*, lower the *gangway*, don his *middy blouse* and *peajacket,* and, if he wasn't too *hard up,* go off *on his own hook* and see whether the *broad-beamed* lady pacing the *widow's walk* still liked him or was just a *fairweather friend.*

Perhaps my father was glad to be forced to be at sea so much as the Depression dragged down Canadian spirits without the lift F.D.R. gave Americans. He romanticised the hardships. Steeped in Conrad and Masefield, he also admired T. E. Lawrence, whose *Seven Pillars of Wisdom* captivated many idealistic young men in the thirties. Lawrence's influence is apparent in one of the articles by "Skipper" MacNeil in the *RCMP Quarterly* describing life aboard the ship he commanded:

> It is a life purely monastic, and of almost ascetic detachment. Calling as it does for a degree of selflessness and of corporate spirit rarely encountered in other walks of life, it holds for even the shallowest character a deep—though possibly unconscious—spiritual significance. . . . When the land dips astern, wind and sun and great expanse of water provide life's background with a vigour and wholesomeness denied most people who have their being in this modern age of asphalt and concrete. And against this background he is absorbed with his shipmates into the unending conflict with nature; and in quieter moments he can turn to the contemplation of the eternal mystery of the sea.

He passed on that feeling to me, though not the taste for Lawrence of Arabia, in his spells at home.

During the war he drank a lot; they all drank a lot. It was a part of their culture. It was Hemingwayesque, as were the sodden moroseness, the black moods, that sometimes resulted.

But he was essentially a cheerful, optimistic character and not an alcoholic. No matter how hung over, he bounced out early in the morning, took a cold shower, and roused us with the bosun's "Wakee, wakee, wakee, rise and shine!" Later, when we were obviously past puberty, he would use the sailor's bawdy addition, "Hands off cocks, on socks!" trying to rile my mother into protesting, "Oh, Bobbie, don't be so revolting! Keep your filthy lower-deck humour for your ships." When he was away she complained that "life among all those rough men has coarsened him." Judging by the half-playful way she protested, however, I think she privately enjoyed it. She was no prude and he was not a vulgar man. But he loved to provoke her and amuse us by saying things like "As my last quartermaster used to say, 'There's more brains in the head of my hammer than he's got in his head!' " with a lewd gesture to suggest what hammer meant. "Oh, Bobbie, you're being disgusting!" my mother would snap, but the same small twinkle showed as when he fondled her too openly in front of us. They were a fond couple, with occasional storms, usually over drinking or money, but essentially very loving to each other and to us.

Heather is another emotive word from my childhood. It symbolised the Scottishness we shrank from parading but cherished. The peninsula on which Halifax is built ends in Point Pleasant Park, a large wooded area left natural, with the relics of seaward defences from the eighteenth to the twentieth centuries. Near the point itself there is a large growth of heather not native to Nova Scotia. The legend is that a Highland regiment bivouacked there, and the seeds from the dried heather in their mattresses took root. That was another romantic connection with Scotland, suggesting a particular beauty from which we were cut off, although we were generations away from people who had lived in Scotland. It was part of that undercurrent of nostalgia many Canadians felt for a homeland they had never seen.

Eyes that had never seen a Scottish landscape would mist up at the word *heather,* the *bonnie purple heather* of the song, as breasts would swell at the name of Bonnie Prince Charlie, who eluded his English pursuers by *taking to the heather.* Even the name *heather mixture* for tweed or knitting wool would make my mother sigh. The word evoked Scott and Burns, whose statues faced each other a few yards from her childhood home. Given a sprig of heather, she would glow with sentiment, as though she personally had been exiled from the Highlands and deprived of their beauty. The sound of bagpipes always lit her up, stirring her blood, and her sparkling blue eyes would say that if she were a man she'd off to war with a lilting kilt and a brave heart. She must have borrowed the mythology wholesale when she married because there was none of it in her background. Her mother's maiden name was Neely, probably Scots-Irish and ultimately related to the Neils or Nialls, but they had been Virginians and Tennesseans since the American Revolution. Her father, Warren Oxner, was descended from Hanoverian Germans who settled Lunenburg County, Nova Scotia. So Margaret Virginia Oxner was not steeped in Scottish lore; but she became a more wistful enthusiast than my father when her name changed to MacNeil.

He was more diffident about it. He left it to his brother, Corty, to explore the Scottish connections and the history of one Neil MacNeil, who deserted his weaver's loom to join the British Army in 1813, and whose son William eventually prospered in Massachusetts. Yet privately I think it stirred Dad a lot, for the sentiment showed now and then.

There was the bookplate depicting the heraldic galley. They gave my brother Hugh the middle names Malcolm David, who had no family connections but were both ancient Scottish Kings. When Michael was born in 1941, my father's ship passed the Western Isles and he dipped some Hebridean sea water to bring back for the christening. It took place in the wardroom of the ship with the upturned ship's bell as a font filled with the water of our ancestors, treated almost like holy water. Everybody saw the romance of that. The newspapers reported it with pictures. During the war Dad brought me, as a present from Scotland, a *sgian dhu,* Gaelic for the little jewelled knife Highlanders tuck into one sock. In 1956, when he moved to London for the Canadian External Affairs Department, my father sent Michael to school at Fettes, in Edinburgh, where he wore a kilt in the Mac-Neil tartan, although there were plenty of schools in England.

Yet he never talked about it the way my mother did. It was one of her ways of infusing us with pride, especially if I was sulky about doing a chore like washing the dishes. "You should be ashamed of yourself!" she would say. "Think of the fine, brave people you come from. What would they think of you? There are no finer people than the Scots." She did not say they always helped with the dishes, but implied that they never shirked their duty, however dangerous or boring. We ate *porridge* (oatmeal); my father's treat on a Sunday morning was a *kipper* (smoked herring) and the house reeked with its uncompromising odor.

I love the word *reek.* I do not know whether it is the smell of kipper that makes me think of *reek* or the word of the smell. Some words are prompts to memory through the other senses. I can close my eyes and re-create the atmosphere of a certain grey spring day in Halifax by remembering the words *Fresh halibut, fresh mackerel!* shouted by the man from Boutlier's fish market, whose handsome, horse-drawn wagon came by frequently. It was elegantly painted, with hinged compartments, which he opened to pull fish from the ice. The words of his cry carry with them the weather of a certain day and the clean smell of very fresh fish.

Reek is one of those strong Old English words that pierce you with their meaning. I think of Kipling's "of *reeking* tubes and iron shards," or the adjective *reeky* that Shakespeare uses when Juliet imagines being shut up in a charnel house,

> with dead men's rattling bones,
> With *reeky* shanks, and yellow chapless skulls.

I have been in a charnel house in London, unearthed when the bombs opened a churchyard in Fleet Street. *Reeky* makes you smell the dead-bone smell. Hamlet, in the scene with incestuous overtones, uses *reechy,* probably with similar meaning, to disgust his mother with the idea of further sex with Claudius, who has usurped her bed as well as the crown. He warns her not to let the King use sex to make her spill the beans; chiding her not to

> Let the bloat king tempt you again to bed;
> Pinch wanton on your cheek; call you his mouse;
> And let him, for a pair of reechy kisses,
> Or paddling in your neck with his damn'd fingers,
> Make you to ravel all this matter out.

Robert Burns uses the Scots variation to describe the wild dance in *Tam O'Shanter:*

> They reeled, they set, they cross'd, they cleekit [linked],
> Till ilka carlin swat and *reekit.*
> [Till each old hag sweated and steamed.]

But as in much Lowland Scots, Burns also keeps the older Germanic meaning of *reek,* to smoke, from the German *Rauch* (*Rauchen verboten*—no smoking). Burns and Scott use *reek,* and *reeky,* a lot for smoking fires and chimney corners.

Reek suggests *rank,* also meaning an offensively strong smell, as when Claudius, aware that Hamlet is catching on, prays, "O! my offence is *rank,* it smells to heaven."

Perhaps it is our modern sensitivity to odours that has sneaked the meaning of *reek* away from steaming, smoking, giving off vapours, to stinking. When someone *reeked with sweat* in earlier centuries, the vapours he exuded were probably not remarked as fastidiously as now.

Both *reek* and *rank* have for me the satisfying directness of the words that come down to us from the Anglo-Saxons and their Viking cousins. You have an example right there in *come down,* both Old English words and quite different in tone and flavour from *descend,* the Latin word through French, which has a softer, more subtle meaning. One has an imperative quality, suitable for orders; the other by its rhythm and sound suggests a more leisurely, even voluntary activity, as in the title of the painting *Nude Descending a Staircase.* It wouldn't be the same if it were *Nude Coming Down a Staircase.* Shakespeare's Richard II plays on the words when asked to *come down* to greet the man who is about to seize his crown: "*Down?* Down, I come" and then "*Come down?* Down court! down king!" We recognise a distinction by making the colloquial noun *comedown* quite different from *descent.* The glory of English is that we can use both, for different effects. *Comedown,* incidentally, would have been quite good Anglo-Saxon. They created words, as we still do, by joining other words together. Only, in Anglo-Saxon, it probably would have been *downcome,* like the German *Untergang* (undergoing, or decline).

The words that survive from Old English, enriched by Old

Norse brought by the Vikings, are still the core of our language, often the first essential words a child learns about identity (*I, me, we, you, they, he, him, she, her*) and possession (*mine, yours, his, hers, ours, theirs*), about his body (*eye, nose, mouth, head, back, front, foot, hand, fingers, toes*), about necessities (*food, bread, meat, drink, water, milk*), about size (*big, little, tall, short, heavy, light*). When he learns

> Sticks and stones
> May break my bones
> But names will never hurt me.

he is saying all Old English words. But if his teenage sister says *gross,* that comes from French.

Perhaps it is because they are such essential words, a survival vocabulary, first imprinted on a child as he feels his earliest emotions, that the Old English affects us so strongly. The words are usually small, like nuts, with strong vowel sounds for flavour and a hard shell of consonants. They are words that can be shouted, sung, screamed in agony, or crooned with a mother's tenderness. And in this day of multi-syllabic pomposities in speech, they have a refreshing directness. They puncture pretension, they dissolve ambiguity, they kill euphemism. They force you to get to the point. They are the words it is useful to turn to when you are saying to yourself, "Hey, what do I really mean?"

The sea was a destination to us. It was somewhere to go, for an outing, a walk. The only real place for the picnics that were a frequent entertainment were the long, empty beaches of Nova Scotia, still empty today. We did not sit on them much to sunbathe and only when very young played in the sand, build-

ing castles with moats for the rising tide to fill. The beaches
had other purposes: to explore beyond the next headland and
the next, learning to run over the rocks deftly, placing each
foot unconsciously; to look for interesting shells; to skip flat
stones; to gather driftwood for a fire. My father was very good
at starting fires in a circle of round beach stones close enough
to balance a kettle or pot. Starting with a tent of bleached
twigs, he had a big fire burning in a few minutes.

We did not go to the beaches only in nice weather. We went
when we went. We enjoyed the beaches as often on grey, cloudy
days with a fresh wind blowing as on days when the sand
reflected a dazzling sun with no wind. More typically, there
was wind and a strong lungful of breathtaking freshness tasting
of iodine and seaweed clean enough to eat.

From my mother came the idea that going down to the sea
repaired the spirit. That is where she walked when she was
sad or worried or lonely for my father. If she had been crying,
she came back composed; if she had left angry with us, she
returned in good humour. So we naturally believed that there
was a cleansing, purifying effect to be had; that letting the fresh
wind blow through your mind and spirits as well as your hair
and clothing purged black thoughts; that contemplating the
ceaseless motion of the waves calmed a raging spirit.

For a child the coast of Nova Scotia was wonderfully rich with
legends of the sea, of shipwrecks and pirates and buried treasure. The heavily indented shore offered thousands of secret
places where ships could hide, tiny coves where boats might
land undetected, with frequent fogs to veil their business. In
the old days it was pirates and smugglers. In my father's day
it was rum-runners. Today it is drugs and illegal immigrants.

Robert MacNeil

Treasure was a word that captivated me. Herring Cove is a dent in the headlands outside Halifax, where after a long fetch of open water, the Atlantic hurls itself against the rocks. There are low, smooth shelves of granite ground out by retreating glaciers and the huge boulders they left behind, hoary with grey-green lichen on the dry side and barnacles on the other. When I was seven or so and Hugh three, my father showed us rusty stains in the granite and said they were the blood of pirates who had fought over treasure. He said there might still be treasure they had dropped. We searched for a long time. Finally my father called out, "What's this?" He wriggled into a narrow opening under the large rocks, and when he crawled out backwards, he held a piece of jewelry, sparkling and glinting in the sun.

"Look at that! Pirates' treasure!"

"Is it really? Really left by pirates?" I asked with big eyes, an eerie thrill creeping over me, sensing the presence of desperate men who might come back. Then, catching a glance between him and my mother, I realised that the "pirates' jewel" was hers. But that didn't kill the mysterious feelings he had conjured up.

"There really were pirates along here, lots of them."

"But is that really their blood?"

"Perhaps. They really did bury treasure along this shore."

"Really and truly?" We said that a lot. I often wish when I am interviewing some politician on television that I could look at him with a child's commanding candour and say, "Really and truly?" I fantasise that one day one of these professional dissemblers will stop and say, "You're right. I'm not telling the truth."

My father was. Nova Scotia is thick with legends of treasure. The most notorious is Captain Kidd's treasure, supposedly buried on Oak Island in Mahone Bay. We heard about it a lot because the Depression gave treasure hunters added incentive. Since 1790 people have been trying to penetrate the mysteries of a shaft sunk in a cliff, but have found only tantalising clues like oak flooring. Rumour and tradition credit the ubiquitous pirate captain with cunningly protecting his blood-soaked fortune by letting the tides flood the lower chambers. Many treasure seekers have died trying to fathom his secret.

I was well prepared to drink up Stevenson's *Treasure Island* when it came along. The opening chapter is still as exciting to me as any book I know. I have only to read the first sentence to feel a little prickle of pleasurable anticipation on the back of my scalp.

> Squire Trelawney, Dr. Livesey, and the rest of these gentlemen having asked me to write down the whole particulars about Treasure Island, from the beginning to the end, keeping nothing back but the bearings of the island, and that only because there is treasure not yet lifted, I take up my pen in the year of grace 17–, and go back to the time when my father kept the "Admiral Benbow" inn, and the brown old seaman, with the sabre cut, first took up his lodging under our roof.

Since my mother first read it to me, I have read the book innumerable times myself. It keeps the boy in me alive. Today I can see that the thrilling story and the antique setting are greatly enhanced by Stevenson's bold, clean language with its high proportion of elemental Old English words.

> I remember him as if it were yesterday . . . a tall, strong, heavy, nut-brown man; his tarry pigtail falling over the shoulders of his soiled blue coat; his hands ragged and

scarred, with black, broken nails; and the sabre cut across one cheek, a dirty, livid white.

I like the taste of the words and the punch of their consonants when said aloud or in the mind's ear. Jim Hawkins, at sea in the tiny coracle, watches the towering ship *Hispaniola* sailing wildly towards him with no one at the helm:

> I was not a hundred yards from her when the wind came again in a clap; she filled on the port tack, and was off again, stooping and skimming like a swallow.

Talk about pleasure! *Stooping and skimming like a swallow* is not only an arresting visual image but the shower of variations on *s* (*st-*, *sk-*, *sw-*) is a gift to the ear.

Then Jim reboards the ship.

> Suddenly the *Hispaniola* came right into the wind. The jibs behind me cracked aloud; the rudder slammed to; the whole ship gave a sickening heave and shudder, and at the same moment the main-boom swung inboard, the sheet groaning in the blocks, and showed me the lee after-deck.

Can anyone read that without excitement? I cannot. The verbs—*cracked aloud . . . slammed to . . . groaning in the blocks*—fill the head with sound and motion. That they are of the sea only adds to the pleasure.

My only trip in a real ship as a boy was when my father took Hugh and me to sea on an exercise called a "night shoot." It was the summer of 1943 and he was temporarily relieved from convoy duty to command a Working Up Squadron training in anti-submarine tactics. The base was Pictou, Nova Scotia, on the Strait of Northumberland, and we moved for the summer to an old pilot's cottage. It sat at the top of a hill overlooking the harbour, with a view out to sea. With a telescope in an upstairs window, I often followed the line of small warships out of the harbour and out of sight. If I focussed the glass correctly, I could see my father on the bridge of his corvette, HMCS *Sorel*. They would be out for a day or so at a time, then back in harbour for a few days.

Compared with our life during the rest of the war, it was a very relaxing time and he was with us all summer. In the evenings, a high-speed launch they called "the skimmer" would bring him several miles out of the harbour to the beach at the foot of our field. Hugh and I would run down the field to the beach when we spotted the launch coming around the light-house on the long sand spit. We would arrive on the beach breathless just as the launch rumbled in, its exhaust throbbing against the swift tidal current that sluiced through the deep channel. A sailor held the bow close to the beach with a boat-hook as my father, sometimes with others he had brought as guests, jumped off, trying to keep their shoes dry.

They would walk up the field to the house, to change out of uniform into tweed jackets and shapeless grey flannels. No one had sports clothes in those days. We had a portable, windup Victrola and they played "As Time Goes By" again and again as they sat in the twilight; my mother, and perhaps other Navy wives, drinking, smoking cigarettes, the dark red lipstick then fashionable leaving bright stains on the cigarette ends. The words of the song played into my dawning envy of their amuse-ments and camaraderie, their being adult.

I was twelve, feeling stirrings of adolescent impatience with my family; stepping into the future with my first pair of long trousers; reading all the works of Horatio Alger in yellow volumes with brittle pages in the attic of a nearby farmhouse; and mooning over Marita Hope, the daughter of another naval couple who brought her for a visit. She and I stole cigarettes and smoked them together behind the barn. With Hugh and a local boy, we played strip poker in the woods. And when she was gone, I was left with a very empty feeling. There was a night picnic for my father's birthday in July, and when I saw a photograph later, I was filled with bitterness that Marita had been invited and I had not. When I complained to my mother that *she* had been included, she said they hadn't known that *children* were to be there. Sometimes one word used innocently like that is like a shot. Subconsciously I must have put childhood behind me. Being lumped with *children* made me angrier still. They might as well have taken back the long pants. I moped around uncooperatively, feeling furious and sorry for myself, as I can see in the sulky photos taken then.

Yet I still acted like a child when my dog was killed. We had a succession of dogs, each called Tigger from the Pooh books. They were all cocker spaniels, bouncy, affectionate, and undisciplined. All came to sad ends, two from distemper, Tigger III from a road accident.

It was a hot day in August around noon; a locust wheezing in the top of a tree made it feel hotter. The tall young man who ran the farm nearby, Lincoln Cameron, walked down the dirt road that led from the highway and told me he had seen the dog. "Must've been hit by the road scraper. It went by a while ago. You'll find him back there," pointing down the road. I ran for about half a mile before I found the dog, lying with his four feet in trotting position, as though he had keeled over in mid-step. His tongue was hanging out and a fly was walking over his open eye. Nothing so close to me had ever died (the other dogs had been put down by vets) and I was filled with revulsion as well as grief. I picked up the dog—already getting stiff—and plunged into the thick evergreen forest, running blindly, dodging the dead lower branches to go deeper into the dark forest, to get him somewhere out of sight. I put him down in the moss under a fir tree and ran back to the road. All afternoon I kept saying to myself, Tigger is dead, not believing it. My mother was away in town that day and came back with my father on the skimmer. Running down to the beach to tell them became more urgent than the pain, the grief transmuted into the self-importance of having real news to tell. This was real news and they took it very seriously.

When he had changed out of his uniform, my father brought a cardboard carton and asked me to take him to where the dog was. Although it was nearly dark, I found the spaniel still under his tree in the deepening shadows. My father was moved. "Poor old chap," he said. He spread out an old towel, lifted the rigid body onto it, and wrapped it up. His competence was soothing, reducing my dread of the dead thing. With some difficulty it went into the carton, which he carried back to the house. We dug a grave under an apple tree and my mother clipped a lock of the dog's hair.

I found it hard to distinguish the gratification at so sympathetic a response from the pain of losing the dog. I think one wiped out the other. My father was so preoccupied and wore such a worried look when he was at home that summer that I had expected more indifferent treatment.

The war shattered the vacation atmosphere one night. I was sleeping on the screened porch of the cottage. Across the water from the Pictou side there was shooting, which woke me up. I listened, but the night was silent again and I went back to sleep. I was awakened again later when an officer opened the screen door to the porch and said he needed to see my father urgently. I went upstairs, crept into my parents' bedroom, and was amazed that the minute I said "Dad" very quietly he was completely awake. He came downstairs and talked to the officer. A nervous sentry on a British ship just in from sea had challenged the skimmer and opened fire when it did not respond. A young sailor whom we had often seen as bowman on the speedboat had been killed. My father took the news impassively and went back to bed, while the messenger walked down the dark field to his boat on the beach. The coldness of the night and the news I had heard made me shiver in my own bed.

One evening later that summer, Dad took Hugh and me to sea overnight. The words *go to sea* were magic ones loaded with years of meaning of where my father went to work, where he was when not at home. Actually to be going to sea ourselves in a real warship, after years of just hearing or reading about it, was the biggest thrill of my life.

We sailed at sunset. As we passed down the harbour, we stood on the bridge looking through enormous binoculars at our house on its hill across the water at Pictou Landing. The ship began to feel the ocean swell. At twilight they let us fire a Sten gun into the water and to shoot off a few rounds from the Oerlikon anti-aircraft guns. The land got mistier astern and the night closed in. It got very dark and cold on the bridge. We were bundled up in sweaters and duffel coats, and kept warm with frequent cups of thick cocoa, the Navy's cure-all.

Around us, the ships went through their exercise, tracking the British submarine that accompanied the group. It submerged and hid. The corvettes turned on their listening devices, primitive by today's standards, and steamed in a pattern, systematically searching a patch of ocean. We heard my father on the bridge giving the commands familiar from books into the voice pipe:

"Starboard fifteen."

"Starboard fifteen" repeated back through the voice pipe by the coxswain in the wheelhouse below.

It is wonderful that in the twentieth century, with all our astonishing technology, we are still using terms that originated with Anglo-Saxon and Viking seafarers more than a thousand years ago. The man who steers a nuclear-powered aircraft carrier is still called a *coxswain,* as was the man (*swain*) who steered a small boat (*cock*). Today's huge ships are still run by *boatswains,* or *bosuns.* The right side of a ship is still known by its Viking function, the side (*board*) on which the steering oar was used, or *starboard,* and the other, the *port* side, because it could lie alongside a dock in port without damaging the steering oar.

When the wheel had been turned fifteen degrees to the right, the coxswain replied, "Fifteen of starboard wheel on, sir."

And my father said, "Steer 225." Just like the Noël Coward movie *In Which We Serve,* which we had recently seen.

"Steer 225, sir."

"Course 225, sir."

"Very good."

This went on for hours, as she crossed and recrossed a piece of ocean totally invisible to me, except for an occasional flash from a signal lamp or the distant loom of a lighthouse over the horizon. It was very dark, although gradually we could see quite well that the sky was a little lighter than the sea. Occasionally my father's face and the gold badge on his uniform cap would be illuminated for a few seconds when he lit a cigarette.

It was hard to follow: the commands, the muttered remarks, the little jokes among the men on the bridge, very relaxed because they were playing a game and not experiencing the real thing. I was getting bored and sleepy, but the climax woke me up. Some time after midnight, my father said sharply, "Stand by!" And to us, "Now be careful! Look over there." And into the tube: "Fire!"

There was a tremendous *bang,* as the forward gun went off with a flash of fire from its muzzle and a reverberating *bung* through the ship, as though someone had banged an oil drum with a sledge hammer. Reeling from the noise, we saw a bright flash far away in the sky; then a star shell blossomed into a glow that illuminated a wide piece of ocean, like a bright moon falling very gently. When it fell a little lower, there, perfectly centered in the path of its radiance, was the submarine, silhouetted on the surface. It was magic.

"How did you know it was there?" I asked, and they all laughed.

"We don't often, just lucky tonight," my father said. I didn't believe that. I thought the whole thing was wonderful.

My father had earned his confidence. The years of chasing rum-runners had made him a good skipper for convoy escort. His previous ship, *Dauphin,* was well known. Each of the ships had a crest painted on its gun turret, many of them personal to the captain. *Dauphin*'s turret showed a Mountie astride a German submarine, like a bronco buster, with the reins in one hand and a revolver in the other. It got a lot of attention when my father, now a lieutenant commander, was decorated by Norway for rescuing the crew of a torpedoed freighter in very

My father with the gun turret badge on HMCS Dauphin

stormy conditions in mid-Atlantic. My mother, Hugh, and I attended the investiture in the admiral's office in Halifax. A Norwegian officer read the citation from King Haakon and pinned the medal on my father's chest while we beamed proudly for the naval photographer. He deserved a medal. By all accounts, it was amazing seamanship to manoeuvre the corvette near the survivors in a North Atlantic gale with German submarines all around. His brother, Corty, who had a flair for the flip remark, sent him a cable of congratulations for the "Scowhegan chest hardware." At twelve, I thought that was pretty funny.

On his next convoy to Britain, my father received a greater honour, an investiture at Buckingham Palace, where George VI gave him the Order of the British Empire. My father was of that last generation of Canadians who felt comfortable as children of the Empire, their Canadian identity subordinated to a higher loyalty. It must have been a supreme moment for him.

Seven years earlier, on a freezing January day in 1936, he had taken me up to the Citadel, the hilltop fortress that dominates Halifax. It was the day of the state funeral for King George V in London. A vicious sleet was driving out of the leaden sky as they fired a long salute of artillery guns. I was five and stood with him in the shelter of a doorway, holding his hand, shivering and feeling the booming of the guns in my chest as well as my ears. He was silent with emotion, paying his respects to the old King in this way when few others were outside. Now, in 1943, he actually went to Buckingham Palace and was congratulated by the new King.

That night, at sea on his corvette, I was awed by the power he commanded in the darkened ship, so mysterious on the vast black sea, with its great throbbing engines and loud guns. This mighty machine, in which 150 men ate and slept, moved about the seas and found its way even in the dark, at a few words from my father. It could go anywhere, his ship and his crew of quiet, efficient men, anywhere on the oceans of the world. If it was dangerous, they would go because he told them to and because they trusted him. My father would know how to get there and come back—and kill Germans on the way.

I can't remember all the questions I asked as we had more cocoa in the wardroom to warm us up. I was excited, dazzled. I went to bed in one of the officers' bunks, and for the first time in my life fell asleep with the sea moving under me, totally happy, knowing that I never wanted to do anything else.

CHAPTER FOUR

We were children who loved winter. I was as impatient for the first real snow to fall in November as for it to melt and be gone the next March.

When the cold came before the snow, we went skating on Williams Lake across the Arm. Remembering her own childhood, my mother put hot baked potatoes in the boots of our skates. After the rowboat ferry ride, one oar almost touching the edge of the ice line on the half-frozen Arm, and the walk up to the lake, the skates were warm to put on and the potatoes cool enough to eat.

When the snow came, we took sleds and toboggans to the old Gorsebrook Golf Course, staying long past dark, intoxicated by rushing down the steep slope of Number Nine hill and climbing up again. In the gardens and in the snowbanks in front of our houses we built large snow forts, reinforced with discarded Christmas trees, the walls wetted to make them icy and harder for invading forces to penetrate. When we were not defending our own forts against enemies, we invaded others (usually when empty of defenders) to tear down their walls.

With the Scouts I went hiking in midwinter, discovering how warm the snow could be when you burrowed down and got a fire of spruce logs hissing and spitting sparks into the cold sky.

Robert MacNeil

Winter made you want to be together; summer was for being alone. Winter made me gregarious at play and in school.

In thirteen years of school I must have spent some 12,500 hours in the classroom but recall very few that conveyed any pleasure in the English language. That must have registered unconsciously. Obviously I learned to read and write and was drilled in the methodical ways of Canadian schools in the parts of speech. There was also copybook handwriting, which I never mastered, emerging with an illegible scrawl.

Some language was presumably being absorbed, to borrow the journalist's term, *on deep background,* so deep I was largely unaware of it. In the front of my mind, *on the record,* were the words of real life, the words that terrified, words that thrilled, words that haunted the imagination; words that were part of the environment, like the smells of Halifax—for instance, the smell of the classrooms at Tower Road School.

On winter days they smelt of snow-dampened wool. The long radiators creaked and hissed under the tall windows. Very little fresh air got in, because the storm windows were attached outside and vented only by three holes drilled at the bottom. So it was hot. Since our britches and socks and the girls' lisle stockings frequently had snow on them, only partially stamped off in the cloakroom, the classrooms took on the not unpleasant odour of moist wool drying. It was stronger when we lined up to take exercise books to the teacher's desk to be corrected. The line formed along the windows against the radiators.

The words *Go to the cloakroom!* always produced an instant of terror. The teachers used the strap, ten inches of some woven rubberised material, doubtless approved by the Halifax Board of Education. Alone in the cloakroom, the woman, exasperated by whispering or passing notes, would say, "Hold out your hand!" You held it out and she gave you four or six wallops.

"Now the other!" and you got the other half. Sometimes they raised the strap as high as they could reach and used all their strength. Sometimes they were quite gentle. Some teachers held your wrist and stood to one side. Others faced you and relied on you to bring your hand back after each stroke had knocked it down. It was a point of honour not to withdraw your hand, but you could let it give a little with the blow.

The beating left your palm and fingers numb and aching for a long time. You couldn't pick up a pencil for ten minutes or so. But anger at being unjustly punished, which happened occasionally, was more than offset by the reward of returning to the class the small hero of the moment. The girls looked scared (they were almost never punished that way) and the boys sympathetic—all very quiet and still. Occasionally a boy came out crying. The whole class would listen in awe, glancing covertly, as he snivelled in his seat. Norman Smith, a brave little fellow whose father had been killed in the war, usually came out with his eyes dancing with mischief. Hugh MacLaughlin, who sometimes tried to beat me up on the way home, blubbered, his saliva forming little bubbles at the corners of his mouth, as he hugged his wounded palms in the armpits of his sweater.

Winter meant boots. *Boots:* that was a word that thrilled. Some boys, whose mothers were square, wore ordinary shoes and buckled overshoes. The overshoes had to be taken off and put on every time the boys went in and out and the buckles broke easily. They encouraged sober walking on shovelled sidewalks, no romping in snowbanks. I suffered with them one winter and longed for a pair of long, leather boots. Going to get them the next fall was one of the most completely satisfying experiences of my life. With the boots on, I wriggled my grey toe bones in the luminous green of the fluoroscope at Wallace's on Barrington Street. The salesman had a pointer to show my mother how much room I had left to grow. No nonsense then about harmful radiation.

The salesman asked me with perfect seriousness, "Do you want them laced in the 1941 way or in the 1942 way?"

It was probably then October 1941. The world was in chaos. My father was off somewhere in peril on the sea. But all reality receded before this question. Embarrassed to be so out of it, I had to admit I didn't know the difference.

The salesman did not exploit his greater knowledge of the world. He took his time lacing up one boot completely, criss-crossing the laces to form a pattern of *x*'s all the way up.

"That's the old 1941 way," he said, then laced the other boot, going under the eyelets instead of over, creating a row of horizontal lines.

"And that's the 1942 way!" I thought it was the smartest thing I had ever seen. Besides, *1941* sounded stale and used, *1942* dashing and bold. I have stuck to the 1942 system ever since—when I remember.

Those boots had one irresistible feature—a small pocket sewn on the outside which closed with a snap fastener. One tiny penknife might have fitted in it or two small marbles, which we called *alleys*. I could never decide just what to put into it, but contrived to open and close the snap absent-mindedly in hopes that the girl across the aisle would die of admiration.

I must have been wearing these boots the afternoon John Godfrey and I were playing in front of our apartment house in a large snowbank. We had dug it out as a fort, with two rooms and passageways to the top. The snow was old enough to have been rained on and refrozen, so it was very hard. Diana Evans, the girl who did actually sit across from me, stopped on her way home from school. She wanted to see the fort, and once she was in it, a game of tag developed, with Diana chasing us through the tunnels, her bookbag bouncing on her back, her cheeks red from the cold and the excitement, and her short blond hair showing under a woollen toque.

"If I catch you, you have to kiss me" was her rule and, amazingly, we complied. *Kiss* was a charged word, supposed to elicit heavy protests. That was our attitude when we played Post Office or Spin the Bottle with Godfrey's sister, Peggy, an impossibly remote and sophisticated thirteen. In the rare movies we went to, if people kissed, we covered our eyes in embarrassment and squirmed until they got back to the shooting.

Whenever we played with girls, games like Kick the Can, the way of showing off was to beat them, then try much harder to beat the other boys. But on this afternoon, as it grew darker and the lighted yellow tramcars rumbled down South Park Street, I suddenly realised there would be more fun in being caught than in avoiding her. And Godfrey must have instantly made the same discovery, because a competition quickly developed over who got taken behind the gate most often to kiss Diana.

The pace was getting hotter, when we saw my mother coming down the street and instantly reversed our tactics, again without discussion, in totally understood complicity. Ostentatiously, we drove Diana away, as though her presence were hateful, throwing snowballs at her and shouting, "Get out of here, stupid girl!"—and other plausible remarks.

"Jeepers, do you think she saw?"

"Cripes, I hope not."

Why we were *scared* of my mother seeing, I don't know, but we were. Of course, when anyone else was scared, we called them contemptuously *scaredy-cats*.

That was the winter I was *scared of* meeting Hugh Mac-Laughlin on the way home, sometimes going around by Tower

Road to miss the corner of South Park and Inglis. I got caught several times and shoved into the snowbank by MacLaughlin. His red nose had a drop of water hanging from it as he leered over me and rubbed snow in my face. I could never fight until I got really mad, and it finally happened with MacLaughlin: I jammed my hand under his chin, making his teeth click together, kicked my knee into his stomach, and rolled over in the snow, punching his face with my icy-mittened fist until he started yelling and ran off swearing.

I remember the oozy mud of the schoolyard in the spring when we made pits for games of alleys; the smell of the birch catkins squashed into the sidewalk on the way to school; the squeal of the tram wheels turning into Inglis Street, the pulsing wail of the air-raid siren as it slowed down to a dry growl just before stopping. I can recall a thousand sensations from those years, yet I haven't the slightest recollection that any of those conscientious and worthy teachers ever communicated anything as vivid concerning English: no enthusiasm, joy, or pleasure. Perhaps they had none. Possibly they felt it was too serious for pleasure. More probably, they showed it in ways I don't remember.

It was no different when I went away to boarding school at the age of thirteen. At Rothesay Collegiate in New Brunswick, I *fagged* for prefects; ran cross-country through the school woods; played soccer; marched with the cadet corps to church behind the bugle band and back to Sunday lunch in the large dining hall and banana cream pie for dessert. I sang terrified solos in the chapel choir; rigged the antenna for a birthday-present crystal set outside the dormitory window to listen with earphones under the bed covers; learned to battle with chestnuts threaded on shoelaces called *conkers* with the English boys evacuated from their school in Britain; listened, straight-faced, when the jovial chaplain, Mr. Keble, gave the ritual "private chat" in his study, his chins spilling over his clerical collar.

"Have you ever noticed when you first wake up that your penis is swollen and hard?"

"No, sir," I stammered, staring at his huge fingers folded over his paunch, the nails the size of clam shells. I had never heard anyone say *penis*. We called it *dickie*.

"Well, you may be a little young still. But it is quite natural when it happens. It's called an erection. Nothing to be worried about, eh?"

"No, sir."

"Sometimes there may be a little discharge from it, in sleep —a white sticky liquid. Have you ever noticed that?"

"No, sir."

"I see. Well, that is quite natural, too. Nothing to worry about."

"No, sir."

"Well, if you do find that you have an erection in the mornings, the best thing to do is think of something else. It will go away of its own accord. A cold shower will make it go away. Is there, ah—anything you would like to ask me?"

"No, sir."

"Anything any other boys doing to you that worries you?"

"No, sir."

"None of the older boys bothering you at all?"

"No, sir."

"Well, that's good. If anything bothers you or if there's anything of that sort you want to ask me about, don't hesitate to come and see me, eh?"

"No, sir."

"Well, off you go, back to your study period, MacNeil. See you on the soccer field tomorrow afternoon."

"Yes, sir. Thank you, sir."

"Good night."

That conversation, which contained no new information but caused me to blush mightily, remains in my memory word for word, while the poets we studied and the books we read that year have left no mark.

One poem—my own doggerel—I can remember in part. It was inspired by the behaviour of the intimidating house master, a swarthy Austrian named Hans Bardach. He carried his pet black snake when he patrolled the corridors at bedtime and occasionally punished boys who persisted in talking after lights-out. He caught me copying my poem in study period and walked around the hall reading it to himself and smirking devilishly over lines like

> And before your thoughts have time to scatter
> Down it comes with a stinging spatter!

Instead of the punishment I feared, he said he wanted a copy and let me use the typewriter in his study to make it. He was a superb skier and it was common knowledge that on winter nights he skied down the hill to the village to visit a certain lady. Perhaps he wanted to show her my poem. But his liberalism had limits. He expelled a boy found with a contraceptive, and paraded the entire house to display the shameful article, held drooping from his fingers like an unclean thing. Forty-five years later they are imploring teenage boys to use them.

As a result, at thirteen I learned the correct word for what we sniggeringly called *French safes* when encountered in parks or floating in Halifax Harbour. I had a chance to show off my knowledge the next year, when we moved to Ottawa. The war was over, my father was back with the RCMP, and I went to a school called Ashbury. In the locker room boys were arguing about what *contraceptive* meant. I was able to end the discussion by proclaiming that it meant to prevent disease: *contra* against, *ception* disease: The next day I was stopped by Curley Powell, the maths master. He was a young man with a sardonic cast of mind, what kids today would call a *smart ass*—a pejorative of genius.

"MacNeil, I congratulate you on your remarkable knowledge of the world—for one so young."

"What do you mean, sir?"

"You were shouting so loud in the locker room yesterday that I couldn't help hearing you. But I think your Latin is a little weak. *Ception* doesn't refer to disease but to *conception*. Look it up."

I slunk away, mortified out of my comfortable assumption that adults didn't know we knew about such things.

Powell was the first person who made me aware that words we said frequently without thinking actually had literal meaning. One late winter afternoon in his maths class, he suddenly said, "God, it's dark in here. It makes me think of that hymn we sing in the chapel, you know, 'By the light of burning martyrs'? Can you imagine that? Isn't that the craziest thing you ever heard of? Just stuck matter-of-factly in the middle of a hymn? Imagine working here with a couple of burning martyrs lighting up the room; probably not burning very quietly . . . screaming and groaning . . . and the smell! What kind of mind could write a line like that in a hymn? Anyway, when it gets dark like this I think, 'Light up another martyr!' "

All that winter, whenever it got dark, he said, "Light up

another martyr. Turn on two more martyrs! We need more martyr-power in here!" We loved it.

One teacher really enthused, radiated joy in his subject—the science master, Leonard Sibley; for a while he made me avid for chemistry, especially the chemistry of blowing things up. That interest was born with my first Lotts chemistry set in Halifax. I made gunpowder from the ancient recipe, but it fizzled disappointingly, while scorching a patch of hardwood floor. Then, patrolling the railway cutting that circled the South End of the city, I liberated half-burnt signal flares and removed the chemicals. Once I picked up a new thunderflash that had not been clipped properly to the track. Opening it with a knife, I found a large supply of explosive powder. I filled empty .22-cartridge cases with the powder, carefully bending the ends over with a hammer—very carefully—then placed them on the tramcar tracks.

Halifax had small yellow trams with single axles at each end and not much springing to smooth the ride. So they rattled and bucketed along, hitting every joint in the rails with a clatter. There was a slight downward slope on that block of South Park Street. One afternoon, I put six refilled .22 shells on the tracks about a yard apart and waited. When we saw the tram crest the slope at the next corner, Godfrey and I hid behind the fence. When the wheels hit the shells, they went off in a loud staccato sequence, like a ship's pom-pom anti-aircraft gun, much louder than a .22-rifle shot. Very satisfying, but the tram did not stop. Perhaps they hadn't heard inside. So I filled a .303-cartridge case with the silvery powder and bent its end over. When the next tram ran over it, the report startled us. Echoing off the houses, it sounded like a mortar. The tram stopped this time.

The conductor and several passengers got out and looked underneath, while Godfrey and I crouched behind the fence not sure whether to laugh or run away in case they came looking.

In Ottawa I found a book on pyrotechnics and wanted bigger and better bangs. Sibley let me use the chemistry lab by myself in the evenings. One night I wanted to try, on a larger scale, an experiment we had done in class—to make chromium metal out of an oxide with a catalyst. You put the mixture in a crucible embedded in sand and ignited it with a strip of magnesium ribbon. The combustion was instantaneous but too small, over too quickly. That evening, alone, I took the largest crucible in the lab and increased all the ingredients proportionately, not realizing that the reaction would be magnified geometrically. There was a flash of white fire which lit up the windows opposite the main study hall. It seemed that the whole school came running. They found me with burnt hands, singed eyebrows, and temporarily blind from the brightness.

Science also gave me language and a strange comfort from the precision of the scientific terms. *Catalyst* meant a definable thing, as did *sublimation* and *precipitation*. *Valence* was a specific property; *meniscus* the surface tension that makes liquids form little hills, an observable effect. Such glimmerings of scientific literacy helped me to grasp one of the real joys of our language: when you know the literal, technical meaning of a word, you can use it metaphorically to your heart's content.

It gives you a different level of confidence to play figuratively with a word if your understanding is rooted in one specific meaning. Most abstract nouns and verbs we have to learn from the arbitrary context of an author or conversation, which often leaves a fog around the meaning. It may take many such hearings to make you comfortable using a word. *Sublimation* is such a word, one with general currency since the popularisation of psychology. *Gladys is sublimating her lust for the minister by polishing the candlesticks on the altar.* Hearing that, you might be a little fuzzy about just what Gladys was doing to her lust—or to the minister. But if you know that, chemically, *sublimation* means heating a solid until it turns into a gas, then having it resolidify but changed by what it has given off, the borrowing by psychology will be much clearer—to express socially unacceptable drives in an acceptable manner, often unconsciously. Both meanings also suggest the *sublime,* a reaching upwards to something purer, more exalted, which may be what Gladys aspired to.

Ambivalence is another good example. Knowing the scientific meaning of *valence,* the ability of one element to be drawn to and combine with another (oxygen and hydrogen to make water), gives sharper understanding and precision to *ambivalence,* in all its wider abstract usages. You need never feel insecure about applying the words in any context, editorial writer or poet, advertising copy or sermon. One more example: *saturated.* We all think of that as very wet, as in a sponge filled with water. The chemical meaning is very precise: the moment in dissolving a substance in a liquid, like sugar in water, when the liquid will absorb no more. Then it is *saturated.* If you want to make the water absorb more sugar, you heat it; when it will not take any more, it is *supersaturated.* Similarly: *oxidation, mutation, precipitation, crystallisation, fermentation, distillation*—I like their exactness, because, secure in their meanings, I feel total freedom with the words.

It is interesting how constantly we plunder new technology and physical science to describe human moods and drives. Chemistry gave us *catalyst,* and *catalyst* became an indispensable word. In any age it is chic to decorate one's conversation with such terms, and easy to overdo it.

Jump-start is an example. *The New York Times* pointed out that the term for transferring battery power from a running car to one that won't start is now being applied to: bills languishing in Congress, a regional economy, a presidential campaign, and *The New Yorker* magazine's advertising revenue. The *Times* found 250 *jump-starts* in its computer file in one year.

Our minds love analogy, which often jump-starts creative thought, and we never stop reaching for fresh metaphors to illuminate the human condition. The tendency only increases as technology envelops us more. Stuart Flexner, editor-in-chief of the new *Random House Dictionary,* estimates that computers have contributed 1,200 words to the language: some, like *read-only memory,* passing from jargon to slang; some, like *interface,* moving from things to people. A classified ad for a manager wanted him to "interface with accountants."

As my interests widened, I had increased pleasure in naming other things accurately. To trees, flowers, parts of a boat, I could add geographical names acquired by stamp collecting and the traditional names of colours learned from painting—*vermillion, rose madder, burnt umber, Naples yellow, Prussian blue, cerulean blue.* For a while I tried using these precise terms in writing and conversation, but discovered that I just sounded affected, because they have no general currency. So I had to use colour references people understand—ruby red, geranium red, brick red, blood red—although all those reds vary in life. My family thought I was much too literal: when I showed them a water colour of a vine-covered cottage, my mother said, "But why did you spoil it by putting in that telephone pole and wire?"

"Because they're there," I protested.

"But you should leave out things that are ugly."

"Why?"

The men teaching English rarely had the fervor of that science master. They tended to serve up the jewels of English verse as enthusiastically as the school kitchen delivered mashed potatoes. But served verse we were, and I do not despise it. There was nourishment in the potatoes and in the verse.

We went through the obligatory English poets, in somewhat the manner we were trotted around museums. Wearily conscientious masters, some obviously dazed that the shipwrecks of life had stranded them upon such barren shores, dutifully unfolded to bored boys in green blazers and school ties the glories of our tongue. Bored? No, probably more distracted, absent on some mental playing field, perfecting a ski turn in the mind, smarting in the loins about a girl glimpsed that morning, merely stewing in the unfocussed yearnings of adolescence.

Few of the masters exhibited a burning pedagogic zeal. I have the text that one of them used, and his marginal notes suggest that he mugged up on Milton, Shelley, and Browning about five minutes before he confronted us. But he had mugged up. Having never attempted it, I can only guess at the tedium of trying to find a chink in the armour of adolescent indifference, to pour in a few drops of nectar. Yet if they thought it was nectar, they had a strange way of convincing us. It came out tasting more like medicine, or something with no taste at all.

Some part of me was parched for poetry, yet when they forced me to drink lots of it, I had no thirst. Whom to blame it on? Wordsworth will do. What a boring man, I thought, as we analysed the rhyme scheme of "Thoughts of a Briton on the Subjugation of Switzerland."

> Two Voices are there: one is of the sea,
> One of the Mountains; each a mighty Voice:

> In both from age to age thou didst rejoice,
> They were thy chosen music, Liberty!
> There came a tyrant, and with holy glee
> Thou fought against him,—but hast vainly striven:
> Thou from thy Alpine holds at length are driven.

What stuff to give teenage boys! It is abstract, lifeless, touches nothing a teenager can understand, and on top of it all, it reeks of mediocrity of thought and expression, of someone writing verse in the spirit of a man sorting turnips. Even the diction is wet. *With holy glee,* for heaven's sake? The Swiss don't do anything with glee, anyway. Later, in college, when deeper immersion in the Romantic period was required of English majors, I got some feeling for the spiritual context Wordsworth lived in: the Romantic Movement, the Age of Revolution, and all that; later still, I spent wonderful days in the sublime land-scape of Wordsworth's Lake District and understood him better, but he still left me unmoved. Many of his august contemporaries felt the same. I wish I had come across Carlyle's devastating opinion sooner: his biographer says he thought Wordsworth

> rather dull, bad-tempered, unproductive, and almost wear-isome, and found his divine reflections and unfathomabilities stinted, scanty, uncertain, palish.

Now there's contempt! But then Carlyle said even worse of Shelley, the greatest lyric poet of his day, whom Wordsworth also dismissed. Even Shelley did not bite into my soul until my twenties. Byron set the young mind dancing, like the eve of the Battle of Waterloo, from *Childe Harold:*

> There was a sound of revelry by night,
> And Belgium's capital had gathered then

Her Beauty and her Chivalry, and bright
The lamps shone o'er fair women and brave men;
A thousand hearts beat happily; and when
Music arose with its voluptuous swell,
Soft eyes looked love to eyes which spake again,
And all went merry as a marriage bell;
But hush! hark! a deep sound strikes like a rising knell!

But even that produced no real combustion in me. The poetic synapses were closed down for adolescence, I suppose. Some poets were clearly less tedious than others. Perhaps some ethnic affinity drew me to Burns and the Scottish Border ballads.

The king sits in Dumferling toune,
Drinking the blude-reid wine:
"O whar will I get guid sailor
To sail this schip of mine?"

Haf owre, haf owre to Aberdour,
It's fiftie fadom deip,
And thair lies guid Sir Patrick Spence,
Wi the Scots lords at his feit.

This experience will be familiar to anyone at school in the 1940s or earlier. There was wide agreement that young minds needed to be loaded for life—*front-loaded,* we might say now, as with interest on loans. We took it matter-of-factly that we were being very heavily front-loaded. Canadian schools, private or public, had curricula set by the provincial governments to prepare students for matriculation examinations. It was what they now call *core curriculum,* with a vengeance.

We used a poetry text approved by the Ontario Minister of Education, to be absorbed at three thousand lines a year. The intentions were admirable. The editor, W. J. Alexander, really understood the perils of forcing poetry into young minds: "The growth of the often very tender plant of poetic appreciation may be repressed by the drudgery of prolonged study. . . . There are poems whose fineness and delicacy are of such a character that in forcing them prematurely on the attention one runs the risk of rendering them permanently distasteful." Don't cast Wordsworth's pearls before swine like me.

That was written in 1924 in a desire to liberalise the regulation requiring "intensive" study of particular poems, by offering more poems for cursory reading. He concluded: "The chief means of arriving at the enjoyment of good music is to listen to it; of painting, to see it; of literature, to read it." Read it we did, groaning and resistant, or pretended we did. I felt like a torpid larva, with all systems on low power, as I waited to break the cocoon of school.

In slighting the men who taught us English, I do some injustice to one man, A. B. Belcher, whose very diffidence had charisma. He appeared each morning, haggard and drawn (we guessed from drink), a strand of uncombable hair falling over his watery eyes, shaky long fingers stained with nicotine, like the lip under his thin mustache, his old tweed jacket buttoned an inch too tight. He seemed always on the borderline of not having been able to get there at all that morning. His handsome but ravaged face wore many sorrows, yet, through all the seediness, he conveyed refinement, even hauteur. For that reason he was nicknamed the "Duke."

I felt some complicity with him and embarrassed for him on his ghastlier mornings, when his voice rasped and his fingers twitched. I assumed that some private agony had blighted his life and he was soldiering on with dignity, like a character in a Terence Rattigan play. I had reason to be tolerant: for three years he gave me progressively better parts in the school play, which he always directed. Then I saw the evening side of Belcher—freshly shaved, hair combed, a silk handkerchief in his breast pocket, handsome in a well-used way, and stimulated to be in female company. The plays were produced jointly with our sister school, Elmwood, a few blocks away, and rehearsals were conducted there. The presence of an Elmwood mistress and the older girls, who were in fact young women, brought out much charm and gallantry. I felt conscious of a rival for female interest.

In the mornings he was again a grumpy, laconic man, looking at us from deep eye pockets; his cigarette reluctantly snuffed out in the last second before class began. Yet, almost perversely, he communicated discrimination and sensibility. You understood what he admired and that, if he did, it must be admirable. Between the sarcasms and the ironies, occasional smiles, the rare warm reading of a line or two, an aesthetic sense leaked through. If you are looking for enthusiasm, you'll find it. Hungry for encouragement, you will squeeze it out of a stone.

Once, in my senior year, rummaging in Ottawa's only second-hand bookshop, I found a copy of Owen Meredith's poems which I bought cheaply for its handsome leather binding and marbled endpapers. I showed Belcher a couple of lines that caught my fancy for the alliteration:

> Far out on the sunless sea
> Where dipped the dancing gulls in glee

He sighed and said, "Yes, it's neat, but a little obvious, isn't it?" I smarted to have my callow taste reproved, but knew he was right. I had bought a second-rate poet, confusing him with the other Meredith—George. Similarly, when he accepted a couple of my verses and a short story for the school magazine, I knew he was being kinder to them than they deserved. But he gave me consistently good marks, and once a handsome Shakespeare as a prize for English.

Belcher also helped to judge the public-speaking contest. There was little competition and I won with some juvenile bombast I am embarrassed to recall, but his verdict as a judge stuck with me: "Thin in argument but impressive in delivery." Or, as many have discovered in television, it's not what you say, it's how you say it. The prize was Fowler's *Modern English Usage*.

Part of the poetry loading was memorisation. Nothing makes a poem yours and so prepares you to absorb it seriously as committing it to memory. Then you can live with the lines intimately, saying those you wish to dwell on to yourself again and again. As you do so, all the subtler poetic devices reveal themselves, the deeper music and the less obvious layers of meaning. If you memorise a poem, even coldly without enthusiasm, the chances are your regard for it will grow. Something learned that well—*learned by heart* is a good expression—taken to heart, becomes part of your mind's ear, another part of the mechanism that lets you weigh words.

In the wisdom of the ancient Greeks, the mother of all the muses, who governed creativity, was the goddess of memory, Mnemosyne. Obviously they thought that if you can't remember you can't create.

Take the famous "Elegy Written in a Country Churchyard" by Thomas Gray. I had to memorise about four stanzas when

I was thirteen or fourteen. The well-worn phrases have come into my head hundreds of times over the years.

> The curfew tolls the knell of parting day,
>> The lowing herd wind slowly o'er the lea
> The ploughman homeward plods his weary way
>> And leaves the world to darkness and to me.
>
> Beneath those rugged elms, that yew-tree's shade,
>> Where heaves the turf in many a mouldering heap,
> Each in his narrow cell for ever laid,
>> The rude forefathers of the hamlet sleep.

Interesting things happen when you *own* a poem like that. It evolves with you as you gain more experience, like a strongly tannic wine gradually oxidizing. However obvious, the felicity of expression mingles with your later experiences, which resonate with the aptness of the poet's vision. The horror-dulled twentieth-century spirit may thirst for musings more existential than *the paths of glory lead but to the grave,* but what modern poet could condescend to a line like *and drowsy tinklings lull the distant folds?*

A learned poem becomes a lens through which you see the world, like the different lenses an oculist drops one at a time when testing your vision, a lens for all the senses, a lens for the soul's eyes.

The overfamiliar, too brightly painted, the too innocent phrase may become an ironic lens—an antique, antic focus on today's reality. It may become part of your personal cliché-avoidance system: the bat-like verbal radar, operating semi-consciously, that keeps you from blundering into the obvious and over-used, unless you mean it facetiously.

It also gives you a mood that helps fix a period in your personal consciousness. Each of us has a personal view of history, a collage of scraps of knowledge pinned here and there on the black curtain of ignorance. In mine, Gray's "Elegy," written in 1751, suggests the time of watery landscapes, washed in sepia tones, in which exquisitely detailed trees and crags dwarf the innocent animals and men; the time when the focus was turning back from classical allusions and abstractions to value individual human beings, humble or grand.

One year after Gray's "Elegy," in 1752, Franklin discovered that lightning was electricity and the French *Encyclopédistes* sounded the first drum rolls in their march to liberal thought. Clive grabbed the rest of India for the British Empire. Only fifteen years later, Jefferson called it *self-evident that all men are created equal*. Gray locked in your mind gives you one psychological fix on the time. So do many others. While the reclusive Gray was ruminating in Stoke Poges churchyard, hundreds of his countrymen were romping through the lusty adventures of Fielding's *Tom Jones* (1749).

A painter's eye memorises, as does a musician's ear. The memory-banks they create are fundamental to their training. Memorising poems gives all of us, amateurs of language, our own memory-banks. Sentimental, lyric, narrative, adventurous, dramatic, bombastic, gothic, facetious, satiric—we heap the phrases up and our amazing brains keep them ready to leap out, bidden or unbidden—all accessible—in milliseconds.

We memorised a lot by a system taught in grade school that made it easy—a system I have used ever since when I need to memorise something quickly. You read the first line and say it without looking at the page. When you can do that, you read the second line, then say it without looking. Then you repeat the first two lines together, and so on, always repeating all the lines you have learned until you can say the whole piece.

Our memory is easily trained but underexercised. I am grateful now that I was obliged to exercise mine extensively when my faculties were young and retained so much. For whatever reason, I have found it much harder, in fact impossible, to retain poems I want to know by heart as I get older. I can memorise them easily, as I can any script, within minutes. They stay in the circuits for two or three days and then are gone.

Another influence sharpened my ear for the music of English verse, the study of German. Permitted to escape from Latin, I was allowed two years of German instead. The instructor was a comely woman, la Señora Pardo de Zela, the wife of an Argentine diplomat. Pretty, perfumed, thirty-five or so, blond hair pulled back like Evita Perón's, sitting impertinently on, not at, the master's desk; discarding her fur coat and revealing an electrifying stretch of nyloned upper knee, she brought a feminine charge to our fusty masculine environment. It propelled me to a different level of attention and I learned some German.

The señora had a taste for poetry. She required memorisation and exact diction, and her enthusiasm awakened in my conscious mind what apparently had been stewing there since early childhood—the magic of poetic sound.

To get on top of German, you cannot mumble or slur it or throw it away as we do our own language in everyday use. You must bend your mouth and tongue to the precise demands of its vowels and consonants, like German spelling, which is so much more consistent than English.

For example, we learned a little song by Heine:

> Ich weiss nicht, was soll es bedeuten,
> Das ich so traurig bin;
> Ein Märchen aus alten Zeiten,
> Das kommt mir nicht aus dem Sinn.

> Die Luft ist kühl und es dunkelt,
> Und ruhig fliesst der Rhein;
> Der Gipfel des Berges funkelt
> Im Abendsonnenschein.
>
> (I don't know what it means,
> that I am so sad;
> A fairy tale from distant times,
> That will not go out of my mind.
>
> The sky is cool and dark,
> And the Rhine flows peacefully;
> The peaks of the mountains sparkle
> In the evening sunshine.)

Elementary stuff, but there are several words whose sound I found exquisite to savour on the tongue. There are no English sounds like: *bedeuten* (means), *traurig* (sad), *ruhig* (quietly, peacefully). Also, no one had ever taken us through an English poem, again and again, insisting that every sound be made clearly and accurately. I could pronounce it quite well after a little practice, and the exercise opened my ears more consciously to the music of words. We had had lectures on alliteration and the subtle internal rhymes of vowel sounds. No one had ever forced us through the fundamentals of hearing them as we had to do to understand the German and pronounce it correctly.

The result was more conscious pleasure in simple German verse than I was yet aware of in English.

Outside the classroom, I was reading hungrily, not for any thrill from the language, but strictly for content. My teenage taste ran heavily to adventure, at sea or in some foreign country. After the *Hornblower* series, I consumed all thirty or so of the

G. A. Henty novels, with titles like *With Clive in India*. When I found an author I liked, I wanted to read everything, as with Jules Verne and Mark Twain. Nevil Shute's early novels hooked me, as did everything by Somerset Maugham and the Richard Hannay novels of John Buchan, starting with *The Thirty-nine Steps*. My particular favourites, read and reread, were the dozen *Swallows and Amazons* books by Arthur Ransome, the *Manchester Guardian* foreign correspondent turned children's author. Although focussed on children, his books are beautifully crafted novels. A close friend, Don McDonald, and I, read the Ransome books so obsessively that we talked in quotations from them. My brothers and I still do; they became part of the family shorthand.

I played soccer, hockey, and Canadian football badly. I was twenty-fourth man on a twenty-four-man football team. Once, out of pity, in the dying light of a raw November day, I was sent in for one play in one game. My hands were cold and I dropped the pass thrown to me. Here beginneth and here endeth the football career. But I had a football sweater with a number, and afterwards, with muscles tingling from a hot shower, I could affect the elastic swagger of the real stars, entering the dining hall glowing and hungry. Those were the days when to be cheered for glories on the football field seemed the pinnacle of human bliss.

I was better at long-distance running and scraped on to the school ski team. But I found my spiritual home, my lifetime apogee of athletic prowess, and a hint of the adulation real school sports stars enjoy—playing cricket.

That quintessentially English game was, even in the 1940s, as foreign to Canada as to the United States. There were a few adult cricket clubs peopled by expatriate Brits, retired officers, diplomats, and West Indians. And it was played by a handful of boys' private schools like Ashbury—still living in some colonial autumn; staffed by British masters exiled by the war and trying to perpetuate the ideals of British public schooling.

Cricket was the most conspicuous anachronism, perverse in cutting a small number of Canadian boys off from their national summer sport, which was baseball. As I later found out, it is a game widely ridiculed by North Americans. You have only to name the fielders (*wicket-keeper, slips, cover, square-leg, mid-off, mid-on, silly-mid-off,* and *silly-mid-on*) to start them laughing. And try explaining the rules!

"Well, you see, there are two home plates called wickets and you have two batters called *batsmen in* up at once . . ."

"Two batters go up at once?"

"No, the *batsmen* are *in* not *up*. And there are two pitchers, called *bowlers,* who *bowl* six balls from either end . . ."

"Two pitchers at the same time?"

"No, they take turns. When one of the *batsmen* hits the ball, he can run or not as he chooses . . ."

"He hits the ball and he doesn't have to run?"

"And there are no foul balls, he can hit it in any direction he likes . . ."

"No foul balls. How do they get him out?"

"If he's run out or caught on a fly like baseball, or if he lets the ball hit his *wicket*."

"What's the *wicket?*"

"That's three sticks stuck in the ground side by side, with two small turned pieces of wood called *bails* laid across the top. If the ball knocks them off, the *batsman* is out. He is also out if he puts his leg or another part of his body in front of the *wicket*. It's called *lbw, leg before wicket*."

"How do you score runs?"

"When the *batsman* receiving the *bowling* hits a ball away from a fielder, he runs *down the pitch* to the other end—"

"What's the *pitch?*"

"It's the playing area between the *stumps*."

"What in hell are the *stumps?*"

"It's another name for the sticks that make up the *wicket*. If the *batsman* steps out of his *crease*, the *wicket-keeper* can get him out by using the ball to knock the *bails* off. It's called being *stumped*."

"So if the guy who hits the ball runs, what happens to the other batter?"

"He runs to the opposite end. If they have time, they run twice or three times. Each time is a run. But if he hits the ball over the boundary on the ground, it's an automatic four runs. If he hits it over in the air, it's six runs."

"How many times do they get up to bat?"

"Just once in each *innings*."

"You mean each inning."

"No, an *innings* is one."

"How many *innings?*"

"Usually only one to a match. Sometimes two, especially if the match lasts more than one day."

"More than one day? How long does it take?"

"Usually all day."

"All day, for Christ's sake!"

"Sure, it usually takes the morning to get one side out and the afternoon for the other."

"All morning! How long can one batter stay up?"

"As long as he can avoid getting out. Often a good *batsman* can make a hundred runs or more, a *century*. Sometimes the best *batsman* can stay in till the end of the game and is never out."

"What do you mean, never out?"

"One man is always *not out*. They say he *carried his bat*."

"That's an awful long time!"

"Oh, they break for lunch."

"In the middle of the game they have lunch?"

"Sure, and they break again for tea in the middle of the afternoon."

"They drink tea in the middle of the game?"

"Yes, with little sandwiches and cakes, and in June bowls of strawberries and cream. Now let me explain the scoring . . . If the bowler bowls six balls—it's called an *over*—with no runs, it's called a *maiden over*. They say he *bowled a maiden over*—"

"Come on! I'm getting out of here!"

"What's wrong? Americans played cricket long before they played baseball."

"We played that pansy game? I don't believe it. No wonder they kicked the British out. *Bowled a maiden over?* Jesus!"

All these terms used to be perfectly familiar to Americans, who played cricket long after the hated British had left. Baseball did not really take over until the middle of the nineteenth century, and the first hardball used was a cricket ball, made smaller. Cricket is the oldest bat-and-ball team game still in existence, popular since the time of Henry VIII.

Except for the accelerated version played on television, cricket is the most leisurely of games—chess on grass, someone called it. People watch as much to see the subtle duel between batsman and bowler, each with a repertoire of fine points to display, as to know who wins.

Curiously, the game which appears so effete to Americans is disparaged by some English intellectuals; they consider cricket the preserve of hearty dolts and village bumpkins. In fact, it is one English sport with no class associations. The game took root all over the British Empire, yet the poet of Empire, Rudyard Kipling, sneered at cricketers as "the flannelled fools at the wicket."

For all that, it is great fun to play. It is often rough: you catch balls harder than a baseball, sometimes hit only a few feet away, in your bare hands—no gloves for fielders. I broke two fingers that way. But it is also a game of nuances. The flat willow and ash bat can be used for a cunning variety of drives, snicks, cuts, glances, pulls, and blocks. To watch a skilled batsman defend his wicket for hours at a time, testing himself against a variety of bowling—fast, slow, spin—is both exciting and soothing.

I loved the atmosphere, usually a beautifully-mown ground surrounded by trees at a distance. I wasn't much good as a batsman, tending under the tension to revert to a baseball swing. But I could bowl and in my last year won the school trophy for the best bowler. Like baseball, that meant getting the biggest number of outs for the smallest number of runs scored against you.

My hour came in the annual match between the school team called the First XI, and the staff, a tradition started when all the staff were Englishmen who played cricket. Now, in 1949, only a few leftover and nearly retired Englishmen still did. The faculty filled out the team with Canadians who came good-naturedly but weren't all as talented. The staff had as captain the deputy headmaster, a rock-hard Brit named A. D. Brain. He had a square, chunky body. When he entered a classroom, his black gown billowing and his pipe puffing, he looked so solid you felt he could have walked through the wall without effort.

Brain taught French, Latin, and Greek, and was the master for the sixth form. He was also the school administrator and chief executioner. Boys called to his office quaked outside because he decided whether an offence merited a caning and, if it did, he administered it. In some schools, like Rothesay, senior boys and any master could beat a boy. Ashbury was more progressive: only Brain had the painful duty, but he was thought to relish it.

Brain always looked at me, I thought, with contempt, because I was Canadian and, therefore, inferior. He was the kind of Englishman whose condescension makes Canadians hate the British, yet fawn on them. Even when I became a sixth-former, prefect, captain of the cadet corps, and other dizzying honours in the tiny scale of school life—the icy, pale blue eyes in the square, Henry VIII face strongly implied that he thought me a shallow, trivial, lazy fellow. Doubtless my own guilt was an ingredient, but he bore down on me very heavily. When I gave up Latin for German, he behaved as though I had abandoned all pretence of seriousness. He was a bully, psychologically and physically. In class one day he asked me a question; standing to answer, I began, "Well, sir—"

Brain snapped out, "Don't patronise me, boy!"

I had no idea what he meant, and when he waved me to go on, I said again: "Well, sir—"

"Don't patronise me, I say!" his voice rising in exasperation.

"Well, sir—"

This time he bellowed. "Are you being impertinent, MacNeil, or deliberately obtuse? I told you not to patronise me."

It dawned on me that my starting with *well* offended him, and when I finally answered without, he huffed and squared his shoulders impatiently and went on. But he never explained.

His classes were dreaded; no one whispered for the hour. Today's schoolboys would call him a *pain in the ass*. We called him, less colourfully, a *prick*.

This was the man who presented himself on the playing field, first in the batting order for the masters' side on the day of the cricket match. It was a very fine day in May. I felt extraordinarily loose and detached about my bowling. When I delivered a ball, I was confident it would go exactly where I intended, as though some invisible hand were guiding my arm.

The entrance of the batsman is one of cricket's highly theatrical moments. It is usually a long walk in his leg pads, with his bat tucked under his arm, adjusting the cotton gloves that have rubber guards to protect the backs of the fingers. Some batsmen scamper in half-apologetically; some walk confidently but modestly; some swagger, some prance. The opposing team size them up psychologically by their gait. Brain came in like General Patton taking command of an army. You could imagine a band playing "Land of Hope and Glory." His vanity about cricket was legendary. He had confided to us (he confided every year) that "if my fingers had been a quarter of an inch longer, I would have been one of the best medium-pace bowlers in England." And, we embroidered, if another part of his anatomy had been a quarter of an inch longer, it would have been doubled.

His boast was in my mind as he took his place at the wicket. I too was a medium-pace bowler. Brain made another ostentatious show of *taking his guard,* asking the umpire to signal when his bat was in the position he wanted relative to the bowler's approach. The batsman then makes a mark in the dust, and that is where he takes his stand to receive the bowling. Brain elaborated the exercise, as cocky batsmen will, slapping his pads, adjusting his gloves, looking around in a leisurely and disdainful way to see how the fielders were placed and, with a final "harrumph!" indicated he was ready.

Our captain was a thin, funny French Nicaraguan named

Henrique Dreyfus. As I walked back to begin my runup to bowl the first ball, Dreyfus whispered, "A dollar if you bowl him out first ball!" I laughed and turned. Brain was a very competent batsman and we all expected him to be in there for hours, knocking up a respectable thirty or forty runs before lunch. Brain expected it too.

He despatched my first few balls smartly, earning three runs. I gave the next ball no particular thought. The invisible hand guided it to a perfect length, exactly between his two outside stumps, with a slight spin that made it break inwards. He put his front leg out in the proper fashion, made the conventional blocking stroke, and hit the ball smartly—straight into my hands. The umpire shouted "Out" and he was out—*caught and bowled,* in the cricket expression: both by me. He was totally astonished. So was I. He straightened up, muttered "Extraordinarily good ball," and walked off the field—the very long walk back—humiliated. My teammates confined their jubilation behind the traditional polite clapping, and Dreyfus said, "Oh, tough luck, sir." But the air was electric with joy. The bastard who terrorized us all was vanquished.

thy right hand, O Lord, hath dashed in pieces the enemy.

I had a blissful moment and then, in the long wait for another batsman, felt some regret for the man whose moment of glory had been snuffed out. Suddenly I knew him: not the monster I believed, but a competent man, not more, hiding his inadequacies by making himself haughty and feared. Life has never dealt me as pure a moment since. I took six more wickets in that match. Is there a life after high school? I must have doubted it that day.

I have played cricket only twice in the nearly forty years since then, but have cherished the game and its absurd language: its *googlies* (balls with deceptive spin), *sticky wickets* (damp pitches that take spin bowling), and *stone-walling* (batsmen who play extra-defensively). *Sticky wicket* has become a general metaphor for an awkward situation and *stone-walling* for being uncooperative. Many cricket expressions developed a wider currency: *hit him for six, off his own bat, stumped, up stumps*, and the Englishman's ultimate protest over bad sportsmanship or unfairness: *It isn't cricket*, or *That's hardly cricket, old boy!*

In her book *Edward VIII*, Frances Donaldson uses one: "King George, who is normally represented as being completely bowled out at this time by his sense of his own inadequacy . . ."

If you define yourself by the language you acquire as you enter different spheres, cricket was another piece of my self-definition.

I entered another sphere at the same time. Canadian schools all had cadet corps in which you marched and drilled with rifles. Because I had a voice that carried and little hesitation in using it, I was made a platoon lieutenant in my junior year.

It is interesting that Americans and Englishmen pronounce that word so differently: the English and Canadian *leff-tenant,* the American *loo-tenant,* closer to the French word, meaning place-taker, he who occupies the place of a superior. I had always assumed this was another bit of British perversity with imported French words, like reducing *Beauchamps,* beautiful fields, to *beecham*, as they call the street in Knightsbridge. But no, Webster's notes a Middle English word, *levetenant,* which must be the origin of the pronunciation. Was it the French help in the Revolution that gave the American military its pronunciation? Did *lefftenants* and *lootenants* face each other at Yorktown? But the Continental Army organised and fought long before the French joined them and colonial Americans would have had the British pronunciation. Americans didn't pick up the French way of saying *general* or *colonel* or *sergeant* but kept the British *gen-rul, ker-nul,* and *sar-junt.* So why *loo-tenant?*

As a schoolboy, I got a taste of the language of command, how different the same words may sound in different mouths. At the beginning of the senior year, the first parade of the cadet corps was called and ranks were assigned. Having been a lieutenant the year before, I expected at least that, perhaps more. But a new instructor was in charge, distressingly ignorant of my expectations. I was made a sergeant, but nursed the grievance privately. For captain, he chose a boy I greatly admired on the football field, Scott Price, an enviably handsome, athletic, even rich young man, pleasantly unaffected by the gilded aura others saw around him. Price was the captain of the football team and an ace at skiing. He had the physical courage to hurl himself into a downhill race course with no holding back. I was much more timid, never brave enough to hit full speed in the steepest bits or the turns. In football, he not only threw, ran, caught, and kicked superbly but charged fearlessly.

Standing in front of the cadet corps, however, he was embarrassed and a little tongue-tied. His commands lacked snap and crispness, so that our drill soon looked slack and ragged. After a few weeks, the new instructor unexpectedly made me the captain and put Price back to lieutenant. Very mixed emotions I felt, privately thrilled, publicly embarrassed for Price. I said something apologetic to him; he took it graciously and appeared relieved.

The first time I took charge, I heard my own voice sound desperately thin and weak in the open air, with no walls to give it resonance. But bellowing out the commands came quite easily. The company began to march, turn, halt, stand at ease, present arms, and all the other things they were supposed to do. It was better than playing soldiers; it was playing soldiers with real bodies who couldn't argue with me. By the authority vested in me, "Attention!—stand at ease!—" I was vain as hell about it, probably comically so to adult observers, marching and saluting by some interior image of myself as Montgomery or Rommel. The Ashbury cadets were tolerantly affiliated with the outfit called the Governor General's Foot Guards. The new Governor General was Field Marshal Viscount Alexander of Tunis, the hero (with Montgomery) of British victories against Rommel, the Desert Fox. Alexander came to inspect us and I nearly split my vocal cords shouting commands.

Saying words in public terrifies many brave men. Charging downhill full tilt in a ski race, diving off the high diving board terrified me. It was easier to be brave with words.

The cadet role seemed to point promisingly to what had always been assumed, that I was going into the Navy. No other careers were discussed and even this was not aired very fully. It was fine with me. It was something to say when people asked me what I was going to do. It sounded not only decisive but brave.

As planned, the year of my graduation from school, I wrote the examinations for the naval college at Royal Roads, in Victoria, B.C. They seemed easier than the Ontario senior matriculation papers which I had weathered. The naval entrance was competitive but I had no worries about it. My room-mate in the last term at Ashbury, Gilles Ross, had the same expectations, with better reason. He was the star of the school that year, athletically and academically, winner of the Governor General's medal, the pinnacle of achievement.

Coincidentally, that summer my parents rented a cottage next to the Rosses' on MacGregor Lake, about thirty miles north of Ottawa. Both families thought we deserved a summer of idleness before the rigours of discipline and study that lay ahead. Gilles and I played on the lake in the day time, and in the small bars of the French Canadian villages, or went square dancing on a platform in an open field, lit with railway flares, with one fiddler and a French caller. I pined for a young lady from Elmwood who had gone back to Toronto, and learned that two quarts of Labatt's Ale made my head spin.

Then Gilles was accepted by the naval college and I was not. I had flunked one of the dozen exams, algebra. My father was in shock, my mother scared. The Rosses next door tried to be diplomatic while very pleased themselves. The sun shone on Gilles; it was very drear and cloudy over my head.

The Depression had really marked men like my father. They were much more pessimistic about life, more fearful and fatalistic than we are. My father had no fear of taking risks himself. The fear came out when it was clear that the only road he had planned for me was blocked. He damned the Navy for its stupidity in rejecting "exactly the kind of boy they need." He damned me for being "careless . . . your head's in the clouds . . . you should have been studying harder," and so on. Mostly, he was morose.

On the weekends that summer, he sat in a deckchair on the dock by the lake, reading, not talking. He moved very slowly. He must have known that his heart was in bad shape, but we did not know, and my own problems soaked up all my curiosity. Why had I failed and what was I going to do?

CHAPTER FIVE

We did not abandon the Navy. Recovering from the rejection by the naval college, my father and I agreed that I should try again. After a year of college, taking maths and science, I would be in a stronger position the next spring. Somehow, money enough to start me at Dalhousie University in Halifax was found, with both grandmothers helping. I was to make my passion for the naval vocation even more obvious by joining the University Naval Training Division, the Canadian equivalent of the ROTC. The UNTD would not only give me a leg up with the naval college application: by attending one parade a week all winter and three months in the summer, I would make enough money to pay for my next college year if the Navy rejected me a second time. If I did all that for four years, I would emerge with a reserve commission as well as a degree!

All these contingencies plotted by Dad with knowledgeable naval cronies were fine with me. They put my future back on some track and it was exciting to contemplate the freedom of college and Halifax, the town of my childhood.

I was chastened. Clearly I had taken on too much the last year and had lost six weeks in the isolation hospital with scarlet fever. Studies got leftover attention. Sobered by my failure, I hit physics and chemistry diligently at Dalhousie and attended the weekly parades at Stadacona, the naval base. But I fell among siren companions, notably a young lady who lured me into "just one play" with the Dalhousie Dramatic Society. My will power dissolved and I was hooked. By the end of the year I had been in four productions and spent most of my spare time hanging around with the theatre crowd. That was when I realised how thoroughly I had been deceiving myself.

For three years I had been acting in school plays, and the fuse, once lit, never went out. Praise for one play begat monstrous ambitions, which swelled with the next. The Navy lay at anchor in some quiet cove of my brain, while the theatre was busy fitting out whole new fleets. I stopped reading about the sea to read plays and books about the theatre. Amazingly, I had hidden all this from myself, continuing to believe that the Navy was where I was headed. Lord Nelson got displaced by another hero.

Tedium often overtook me in my school years; perhaps that's how well-treated slaves feel. Between home and school, life seemed all burdens and no choices. Someone in authority always commanded my attention or presence. The time was so constructively filled, one obligation slid so smoothly into another, that I couldn't escape into my own mind until bedtime. Even what might give pleasure was often covered with a pall of duty.

There was an exception on a winter afternoon in 1948 and it changed my life. I didn't find God but I found William Shakespeare, a piece of God's work so extraordinary that he comes close to divinity itself.

How weary, stale, flat, and unprofitable
Seem to me all the uses of this world.

The words hit me with a flash of recognition. There, exquisitely
put, was the enervating mood, the despair so painful-delicious
to seventeen-year-olds that often visited my late adolescence.
Never before had there been such instant connection between
something I felt and a set of words to describe it—giving me
both distance from my feelings and better understanding of
them. The words made me two people at once, the person
observed and the observer. The ironic cast of Shakespeare's
words released me a little from the prison of my self-absorption,
and hooked me into a wider, grander scheme of things. They
made me larger, freer.

I had received implants of Shakespeare before then, much
as an inert doll gets its sawdust stuffing. When no one was
looking, gobs of *Henry IV, Part I, The Tempest,* and *Julius
Caesar*—previously packed into me—had just trickled out
again.

The play set that year for the Ontario senior matriculation
was *Hamlet* and the English master, Mr. Belcher, took us to
see Laurence Olivier's new film version. From the first grinding
chords of the opening music over the battlements of Elsinore,
its dark walls washed by the angry sea, I was bewitched.

So perfect was Olivier's diction that you heard every word;
you could imagine you heard even the commas. The words
made kinds of sense I had never encountered. They carried the
plot and character, certainly. They conveyed emotions appropriate to the scenes and a lot of humour—but something more.
They lifted me to a not quite earthly plane, transported me for
long moments into another realm of time and being; a poetic
world, in which the flow of words controlled the weather and

the climate, the cast and light of the day, and the mood of the people.

> 'Tis now the very witching time of night,
> When churchyards yawn and hell itself breathes out
> Contagion to this world:

The sounds of the words put a precious mist over reality and I was inside the mist. I was excited by the sword-play, titillated by the love scenes, amused by Hamlet's ridicule of the courtiers, but I was enchanted by the words and Olivier's way of speaking the meter so that it sounded both poetic and conversational.

I went back to school in a daze and got out the text of *Hamlet*. Almost without effort, a passage read a few times shifted itself into my memory. I had memorised it without trying to. It was Hamlet's first substantial speech, to his mother, that begins *Seems, madam! Nay, it is; I know not "seems."* Once they were in my memory, the more I said the words to myself and thought about their meaning, the more pleasure they gave me.

There were simple effects, like the three *k* sounds running together in *inky cloak,* arresting because they arrest the tongue. There was the sarcasm in the overblown images he tosses at his mother in exasperation because she reads his grief too lightly.

There was a level on which the late adolescent in me responded to Hamlet, thrilled by the power of words he had to tell the world off: such a quiverful of word weapons with which to flick, or pierce, or smash those who frustrated him because they controlled him.

> Bloody, bawdy villain!
> Remorseless, treacherous, lecherous, kindless villain!

What ammunition! I felt intuitive kinship with this Prince who wavered between the callow and the manly, petulant and philosophical, self-pitying and self-mocking.

What youth has not felt that *the time is out of joint?* But until he said it, who thought of such a neat and startling image? *The time is out of joint.* No wonder people have used it for four centuries. What late adolescent has not lived weeks when

> the native hue of resolution
> Is sicklied o'er with the pale cast of thought . . .

For me at seventeen, Hamlet was the great teller-off, an angry young man for all seasons; a very young man in spirit, who escapes from action by talking and hates himself for it.

> Why, what an ass am I! This is most brave
> That I, the son of a dear father murder'd,
> Prompted to my revenge by heaven and hell,
> Must, like a whore, unpack my heart with words,
> And fall a-cursing, like a very drab,
> A scullion!

Yet he goes on *unpacking his heart with words,* with an extraordinary list of things—apart from the murder of his father—that annoy him: drunkenness and debauchery; actors who overact; people who mistreat underlings; proud men contemptuous of others, insolent officeholders, delays of the law, unworthy people who scorn those with merit who don't push themselves; unnecessary pomp, and the foppish affectations of courtiers.

Very young men are often vociferous about such things, as older men are more relaxed, resigned to an imperfect world. But they fall a little oddly from the lips of the Crown Prince of an important country who has finished his studies and is waiting to be King. What need had he to catalogue *the law's delay, the insolence of office . . . the proud man's contumely?* to consider them grounds for suicide? What officeholder would have dared be insolent to Hamlet, at least before he appeared mad?

Hamlet also dwells with disgust on the carnality of love-making, painting gross pictures like *the rank sweat of an enseamed bed* to make his mother ashamed of her behaviour with Claudius, and he lashes out at women generally for frailty, inconstancy, dishonesty, even for using make-up.

T. S. Eliot, who thought *Hamlet* an artistic failure, complained that the Prince is "dominated by an emotion that is . . . in *excess* of the facts as they appear." Eliot said the play, "like the Sonnets, is full of some stuff the writer could not drag to light, contemplate, or manipulate into art."

Others have intuited that "stuff" to be the pith of Shakespeare himself, and that Hamlet was the character in which he most revealed it. Before Eliot, Frank Harris argued persuasively that "whenever Shakespeare fell out of a character he was drawing, he unconsciously dropped into the Hamlet vein." In *The Man Shakespeare and His Tragic Life-Story,* Harris finds many of Hamlet's traits—the habit of talking to himself, that pensive sadness and world weariness, the melancholy and contemplative spirit, the loving sympathy, the bookish phrases, the gentle heart, the quick intelligence, the irresolute man driven to violent action, and, above all, the incomparable lyric gift—in Romeo, in Jaques in *As You Like It,* in Macbeth, in the Duke in *Measure for Measure,* in Posthumus, the hero of *Cymbeline,* and in others.

Scholars may argue endlessly about such things, as they do with great passion about the identity of the man who wrote the plays. What cast a spell over me that day in 1948, and has held me ever since, was the Shakespearean sensibility: that mysterious and compelling bitter-sweet attitude to life of which Hamlet is one intoxicating expression.

Sometimes, when young, you have a dream of something you have not yet experienced and on waking feel set ahead, as though the player controlling your life had moved you several spaces on the board. You have a strong feeling of having been advanced in experience. That was my feeling on encountering *Hamlet*. Knowing him, I felt more worldly, advanced a space or two.

Like millions before me, the more I looked, the more I found, and forty years later, the more I look, the more I still find; better recognising that this play has become a thought bank for English, more quoted than anything but the Bible. Think of that: just this one play, only one of thirty-seven, gave such effective voice to so many ideas and feelings human beings encounter that, four hundred years later, Shakespeare's are the words that come to our minds to express them.

Masefield said, "The play is a part of the English mind for ever." He was too insular: Hamlet is a part of the *world* mind and part of the common speech of people who speak English all over the world. Millions who have never read it and never seen it performed yet speak it from day to day in everyday phrases like:

> *'Tis bitter cold*
>
> *I am sick at heart*
>
> *Not a mouse stirring*
>
> *It started like a guilty thing*
>
> *So much for him*
>
> *This too too solid flesh*

That it should come to this!

It cannot come to good

In my mind's eye

More in sorrow than in anger

All is not well

Neither a borrower, nor a lender be

To thine own self be true

More honoured in the breach than the observance

I could a tale unfold

O my prophetic soul!

Leave her to heaven

Brevity is the soul of wit

More matter, with less art

What a piece of work is a man

The play's the thing

To hold the mirror up to nature

The lady doth protest too much

I must be cruel, only to be kind

We know what we are, but know not what we may be

Rosemary, that's for remembrance

The rest is silence

Those are only the often-used phrases from *Hamlet* that sound most colloquial today, leaving those equally familiar but with a more literary ring:

Wordstruck

The bird of dawning singeth all night long

Frailty, thy name is woman!

The primrose path of dalliance treads,
    And recks not his own rede

Give thy thoughts no tongue

Something is rotten in the state of Denmark.

There are more things in heaven and earth, Horatio,
    Than are dreamt of in your philosophy.

'Tis true; 'tis true 'tis pity;
    And pity 'tis 'tis true.

Man delights not me; no, nor woman neither

'Twas caviare to the general

To be, or not to be: that is the question

The slings and arrows of outrageous fortune

To die: to sleep: No more

To sleep: perchance to dream

Thus conscience does make cowards of us all

Like sweet bells jangled, out of tune and harsh

To have seen what I have seen, see what I see!

Give me that man that is not passion's slave

O! my offence is rank, it smells to heaven

Lay not that flattering unction to your soul.

How all occasions do inform against me

When sorrows come, they come not single spies,
    But in battalions

Sweets to the sweet: farewell!

There's a divinity that shapes our ends

Absent thee from felicity awhile

Now cracks a noble heart. Good-night, sweet prince,
  And flights of angels sing thee to thy rest!

Obviously, I saw only a fraction of this on first encountering *Hamlet* that winter. I knew how he spoke to me at seventeen. He was intriguingly mysterious and yet perfectly understandable. I understood him, as every sympathetic person does, in my heart, while delighting in the ultimate mystery that has intrigued the world for four centuries. The drug that altered the mind and made me understand was the ceaseless flow of words, so cunningly, so deliciously combined.

  How weary, stale, flat, and unprofitable
  Seem to me all the uses of this world.

I said that—and said it—and said it, savouring the cadence, the flow of sound, with the *t*s clicking and spitting contempt. In the first line, look at the striking effect of juxtaposing Old English, *weary, stale, flat,* with the French *unprofitable*. It changes the rhythm, colours the tone, and crowns the line emphatically. The same effect comes in the words

  O! that this too too solid flesh would melt,
  Thaw and resolve itself into a dew;

The French, Latinate, words often have more syllables and softer sounds, consonants less clipped than the Teutonic or Scandinavian sounds. Our language marries these spirits of the North and the South; spirits from the realms of dark, cold winters and icy seas, where action makes the blood run hot enough to survive; and those from the South, where nature is kinder, where vines and fruit may flourish. All of us descended from these people carry the opposing strains in us, and all of us who use English can feel them. Unconsciously, as we speak and write, we are blending the two. In what measure we blend them governs the effect we produce.

Hamlet gave me more forcibly the idea of words: he made me aware that I had word-hunger and a strong desire to satisfy it. I craved more of the drug, for myself privately, but also to put some of my own noise upon the world—to show off.

It was a few months before graduation and the impending naval fiasco. I was again a boarder at school, my parents convinced I needed to be freer of home distractions as the final exams approached. In breaks from studying I would roam the halls invading the studies of other seniors and spouting whatever chunks of poetry I had just learned.

Olivier had cut *O, what a rogue and peasant slave am I!* I gobbled that one up with all its ranting curses and made a nuisance of myself declaiming it on the slightest provocation. When the LP recording of selections from *Hamlet* came out, I listened so hard that I memorised every inflection and intonation Olivier used. When I later heard other recordings, John Barrymore's, for example, I thought them greatly inferior.

But the play to be performed at school that spring (1949) was Noël Coward's *Hay Fever*.

I was already immersed in the theatre, devoting all the time I could steal and more than was profitable for my other activities that year. On Friday nights I went to the English Stage Company, to see the young Christopher Plummer in a weekly repertory of standard plays. The rest of the weekend, when I could get away with it, I hid myself in the magical darkness backstage at the Ottawa Little Theatre, to be a stagehand or extra prop man or scene painter—anything, the most menial task, that permitted me to breathe that charmed air. To emerge from the stage door into prosaic daylight, if only to get a sandwich down the street, seemed romantic because I was coming from the theatre and going back to the theatre. When the stage was empty, often late at night, with the curtain open and a work light on, a friend and I would play scenes, or I would unload my newly-learned speeches from *Hamlet,* testing my voice production and diction to hear the consonants coming back from the rear wall.

Others who have been stage-struck will recognise an acute and hopeless case. It was like being in love. I rushed breathlessly, dropping anything to be there. I dawdled and prevaricated, made constant excuses to myself, and left only when I was torn away.

I was infatuated with the ambiance, such a contrast to a formal boys' school: the easy intimacy between the sexes, the lack of prudery, the informality of clothing and conversation; the (to me) unaffected references to sex; the uninhibited jokes about personal matters. The very air in the green room, a certain musty perfume coming from old make-up and costumes faintly redolent of the bodies that had worn them, that very air was sexy in an abstract way.

It took me a while to realise that I was not the only one who felt it. Even the older people who had been coming for years arrived with a little extra juice that did not flow in their lives outside the theatre. Eventually I realised that the very unaffectedness about sex, for example, could be an affectation itself and that such determinations become collectively an aphrodis-

Acting at the Ottawa Little Theatre

iac. There was an occasional actress you kissed in rehearsals who responded with unmistakeable private invitations.

Even if older and more worldly, many of these people were escaping from something sad or tormenting or just unfulfilling, to the cheerfulness, companionship, romantic opportunities—all rationalized as hard work. Indeed, they worked harder than I had ever seen. For the first time I saw people working at what they loved to do. I could not imagine there was any other way in which people could earn their living and so love doing it. All the models I had of adult work life carried an implied grudge: from my father, back in a peacetime routine, going off to work in the morning, to the schoolmaster's professional disdain.

There was some theatrical blood in my family. My father's mother, Emily Auburn Stewart, was an actress, mostly in musicals, before she married my grandfather Robert Ware MacNeil, who perhaps first saw her on stage. He may have picked up love of the theatre from his mother, Frances Ware MacNeil. I have part of a diary she kept in Boston in 1863, recording her infatuation with the celebrated Edwin Booth. She notes every time he played there, how she entertained him at home, and the occasional appearance of his brother, John Wilkes:

> I am afraid J. W. Booth is somewhat inclined to be rowdy. Mary Osborn met him the other day with his hat on one side, soiled linen with a diamond pin, and I'll be bound he had checked trousers and his hands in his pockets. Well, well, I never supposed he was so refined and gentlemanly as my dear Edwin.

Her daughter-in-law, my grandmother Emily, had a brother and an uncle working in the theatre, one as a stage-manager, travelling on the popular circuit, Toronto–Montreal–Albany–Hartford–Boston–New Haven–New York–Baltimore–Washington. Passed down from them I have Henry Irving's prompt copy of *Macbeth*, with hand-written stage directions. My Uncle Corty, Dad's younger brother, was a regular performer with the Montreal Repertory Theatre, toured with them to entertain troops during the war, and appeared in some National Film Board movies.

These connections were not trotted out much at home—my mother, in particular, thought the theatre raffish—but they helped to explain why I felt so comfortable in that world.

My deep immersion meant another batch of jargon, and I learned in a personal way how group language includes and excludes; how much it is part of belonging to a group to speak their special speech; how people eager to feel *in* compete with others to know the correct term. It was part of the subtle competition in these amateur ranks to be thought more experienced, even professional. So there were phrases dropped like ". . . the best West End production of the *Shrew* in years . . . It was a great warhorse in provincial rep . . . You remember that revival of *Charley's Aunt* on Broadway . . . Think how the Lunts would do it, dear . . ." and so on. Dying to belong, I eagerly lapped up and freely tossed around all the in-sounding terms I could:

"It goes behind the *tormenter*."

"You mean the *teaser*."

"Oh yes, of course. Isn't that funny, I keep mixing them up." Funny? Try mortifying!

"Well, how would it be if I were to *come on*, like this but *bigger, cross downstage* of Judy, then *cheat up* to Thomas."

"Very nice, dear, but if you don't mind, *I'll* direct the scene."

So special was the atmosphere of belonging, so strong the condescension to outsiders, that I felt like someone at a dinner party with Nancy Mitford, trying to catch what was U and non-U, fearing to call a *napkin*, God forbid, a *serviette*.

Were they so insecure, or was I just adolescent and over-anxious? Including, excluding: what an effort we make to adopt the tics of speech that will make us feel closer to someone, to some group. How quickly we pick up a cute expression or slang phrase a loved one uses, holding it like an intimate possession, repeating it in the right mood, or to create the right mood, to be more intimate. Without noticing, we do that at work, to ingratiate ourselves, to be buddies, one of the guys. Words are gates and fences.

Much theatre talk is no longer exclusive to that life. Like the sea, the stage is a rich source of metaphor for people who never go near it.

We talk of *standing in the wings, upstaging someone, taking center stage, playing a major role, a leading role,* or being *walk-ons, bit players,* or *spear-carriers. Backstage, onstage, offstage* have wide non-theatrical meanings, as do *stage whisper, playing to the gallery, over-acting, hamming it up, drying up, it's curtains, final curtain, curtain calls, entrances and exits, exit lines,* and *laugh lines. If it works, they keep it in* and *play it for laughs.* We *stage-manage* board meetings, *bring down the house, raise the roof, paper the house,* have a *hit* or a *flop, play the heavy,* or *seek the limelight.* Some people are *quick studies* and make *quick changes,* some remain *understudies* and never get *a big break with their name in lights,* but are *prima donnas* all the same.

The theatre is not only glamorous to people outside, it responds to a simple, and ancient, psychological need: to see human life represented, literally *played.* Children act out their fantasies and fears; adults like to see others act them out. According to Jung, our very dreams are theatre, "where the dreamer is at once, scene, actor, prompter, stage manager, author, audience, and critic." In waking life all people do some performing, and know it.

Away from the theatre I snatched anything to read that would transport me back into that world. I consumed more books in that genre than I was reading for my courses: all the plays, biographies, and theatrical reminiscences I could find.

My parents suggested diplomatically that Noël Coward's exotic style of life might not be the best model for a wholesome young Canadian, but I put that down to their irredeemable provincialism. How could they understand that I needed to gulp sophistication, so much had their upbringing starved me of opportunities to become worldly? Deep in the breezy cattiness of Coward's *Present Indicative,* I felt transported from the uncouth outpost to which fate had temporarily consigned me. It did strike me, passingly, that Coward's friendships with women, like Gertrude Lawrence, were consistently superficial, but as close friendships with men were discreetly omitted, what did I know?

I emerged from the "run" of *Hay Fever* (three nights) as Coward might have after a year in the West End, world weary, needing some new stimulus before another bout with the muse. At home over Easter, when I briefly affected a dressing gown, ascot, and cigarette-holder around the house, my parents were marvels of sarcastic restraint.

Olivier's earlier film of *Henry V* had also come to Ottawa and I found the language as mesmerising as *Hamlet*'s. Soon I had memorised all the speeches of the Chorus and the King.

The English Prince of *Henry V* (written at the same time as *Hamlet*) is the Danish Prince with reversed polarity, as they say in television, when they can make a positive negative or the black white at the touch of a switch. Character apart, the language is glorious, not only the speeches in which the King lashes his depleted troops into a patriotic frenzy, but the moments of inspired scene-setting given to the Chorus. My favourite is the description of the French and British armies encamped, waiting for dawn and the Battle of Agincourt, a word picture and a sound poem of extraordinary delicacy and mood change.

First, there is the line to re-capture the attention of an audience as the new act (IV) opens, with its commanding and arresting *t* sounds,

> Now entertain conjecture of a time

a line that can be bellowed over the distractions, to command quiet for the sensuous and tangible images that follow:

> When creeping murmur and the poring dark
> Fills the wide vessel of the universe.

Think of *creeping murmur* and the way small noises travel outdoors at night. Think of *poring dark,* an utterly Shakespearean leap of meaning, of darkness demanding strained attention, darkness to be *pored over* and peered into, yet darkness itself *poring over* the landscape, giving its attention to every atom of the surface of the earth, yet further suggesting a dark so thick it is liquid and the universe a vessel it has filled, and so a pun on *pouring*. To pick it apart scatters the quicksilver of Shakespeare's thought, but you have only to read it again whole, and aloud, to bring it back. Now another image for night:

> From camp to camp, through the foul womb of night,

Then a series of sounds, as explicit as directions for the sound-effects man in a radio play, yet suffused with the magic of night, and startlingly original in diction:

> The hum of either army stilly sounds,
> That the fix'd sentinels almost receive
> The secret whispers of each other's watch.

The first line is magical to me. What possessed him to use the noun *hum* for the muted sounds of two armies largely asleep? Whether you or I have ever heard anything like it, we recognise instantly how inspired it is; it conveys not what the two armies might sound like but, more important, what Shakespeare wants us to feel they sounded like.

Then he mutes it again, with *stilly sounds,* like a pianist applying the soft pedal. The words almost require a speaker to whisper them, so suggestive are they of quiet. Then, after a brief, visual image,

> Fire answers fire, and through their paly flames
> Each battle sees the other's umber'd face:

come a set of different sounds—sharp, tormenting—each a warning of the slaughter to come:

> Steed threatens steed, in high and boastful neighs
> Piercing the night's dull ear; and from the tents,
> The armourers, accomplishing the knights,
> With busy hammers closing rivets up,
> Give dreadful note of preparation.

But he lets these alarms subside, as they might in the fitful sleep of a worried soldier.

> The country cocks do crow, the clocks do toll,
> And the third hour of drowsy morning name.

The construction *cocks do crow* and *clocks do toll* reintroduces a sleepy rhythm: *And the third hour of drowsy morning name* is practically a yawn.

Then follow contrasting descriptions of the *confident and over-lusty French* and the *poor condemned English,* all to set the stage for *A little touch of Harry in the night,* when the King visits his frightened and outnumbered troops: scenes heavy with the tenderness commanders know for the men they are about to commit to battle. Harry's speech rises from brisk prose with the common soldiers to a philosophical musing worthy of Hamlet:

> Upon the king! let us our lives, our souls,
> Our debts, our careful wives,
> Our children, and our sins, lay on the king;—
>
> What infinite heart's-ease must kings neglect,
> That private men enjoy?

Then, as the pace begins to quicken and the dread battle approaches, on to perhaps the most thrilling invitation to glory ever written:

> This day is call'd—the feast of Crispian:
> He that outlives this day, and comes safe home,
> Will stand a tip-toe when this day is named,
> And rouse him at the name of Crispian.
> He that outlives this day, and sees old age,
> Will yearly on the vigil feast his friends,
> And say, "To-morrow is Saint Crispian":
> Then will he strip his sleeve, and show his scars,

And say, "These wounds I had on Crispin's day."
Old men forget; yet all shall be forgot,
But he'll remember, with advantages,
What feats he did that day. Then shall our names,
Familiar in his mouth as household words,—
Harry the king, Bedford and Exeter,
Warwick and Talbot, Salisbury and Gloucester,—
Be in their flowing cups freshly remember'd.
This story shall the good man teach his son;
And Crispin Crispian shall ne'er go by
From this day to the ending of the world,
But we in it shall be remembered,—
We few, we happy few, we band of brothers;
For he to-day that sheds his blood with me,
Shall be my brother; be he ne'er so vile,
This day shall gentle his condition:
And gentlemen in England, now a-bed,
Shall think themselves accurs'd, they were not here;
And hold their manhoods cheap, whiles any speaks,
That fought with us upon Saint Crispin's day.

Can the faintest heart, the most unmilitary man, read that and not feel for an instant the courage rise in his blood, and imagine himself hurling his life after such a leader? I cannot.

Hamlet and *Henry V* had opened for me a door which then never closed. My immediate interest was histrionic: to get a chance to say these stunning words in public, for the sheer vainglorious pleasure that makes any actor want to strut his stuff: to show off and to be admired and applauded for it. Even before what it means, or how important a play is, an actor thinks, Wow! I could sound great saying that! Let's see, how many scenes am I in and how many lines are there?

At Dalhousie, what first lured me from my spartan naval path was the knowledge that they did Shakespeare each year. After some auditions, they cast me as Cassio in *Othello*. That was an ample part for my small experience. I handled it competently and was well received, and thus set up for greater things in my sophomore year.

If possible, given the size of my theatrical ego, it was as gratifying to sit and listen and watch the great scenes of the play in which Cassio does not figure, for the subtleties of the characterisation and the sublimity of the verse. I attended every rehearsal, whether they called my part or not, and my ears soaked up the words. To be attentive in a production of Shakespeare is almost to ingest that play. You work with an acting edition that is full of notes on the characters' motivations drawn from some of the great interpretations of the past. You hear director and actors discussing the minutest shades of meaning. If the main parts are well cast, you hear the lines beautifully spoken, dozens of times. So I did with *Othello*. It is easy to say you like the stuff but hard to say why. I start with the rhythm—the majestic, rolling cadences of Othello's formal lines,

> Most potent, grave, and reverend signiors,
> My very noble and approv'd good masters,—

When you say that aloud, say it deliberately, testing the weight of the syllables it is appropriate to stress and the lightness of those unstressed, you feel the musical proportions of the lines. In the first,

> Most potent, grave, and reverend signiors

the silent metronome in your mind counts the beat as one-TWO, one-TWO, one-TWO, and the second line,

My very noble and approv'd good masters

as one-two-THREE, one-two-THREE, and so on, the skipping rhythm of the second line picking up the pace as the vowel sounds and more clipped consonants contrast with the long full vowels and softer consonants of the first. The honoured general, having flattered the dignity of his civilian bosses, is now impatient to get on with it. In the different cadences one may even suspect a little sarcasm.

Such analysis apart, the damn words just sound good together: the velvety unction of

Most potent, grave, and reverend signiors,

and the clipped, impatience of

My very noble and approv'd good masters.

The words fall together in a way that leaves a pleasant aftertaste on the palate that makes you want to say them again to savour it; as when Othello, the black middle-aged general, tells how he wooed Desdemona, the sheltered white daughter of a Venetian nobleman:

Rude am I in my speech,
And little bless'd with the soft phrase of peace;

And therefore little shall I grace my cause
In speaking for myself. Yet, by your gracious patience,
I will a round unvarnish'd tale deliver
Of my whole course of love . . .

This stuff flows out of Shakespeare as wine from great vineyards, unique even at its least distinguished moments. Besides the richly sensual quality of Shakespeare's language, there is delight for me in the odd usage, the stunningly apt but odd adjective. His way of putting two words together can still be fresh and startling four centuries later, because the dissonances, though familiar, remain pleasantly dissonant, astringent compared with the sweetness of older harmony.

In the opening scene of *Othello,* the unfortunate Roderigo tells Desdemona's father that she has been transported

> To the gross clasps of a lascivious Moor

the words dripping with Roderigo's sexual-racial jealousy and frustrated hopes. But what a combination: *gross clasps!* What a picture, if the slow-witted father had not had picture enough from the pitiless Iago, a few lines before:

> I am one, sir, that comes to tell you, your daughter and the Moor are now making the beast with two backs.

In the next scene the father, Brabantio, says that Desdemona shunned other suitors whom he calls

> The wealthy curled darlings of our nation.

Curled darlings pairs two common words to delicious effect, arresting visual images, yet mocking, suggesting the annoyance rich old men often show for the pampered youth of their class. Such insights coupled with bold word use flash by constantly. In the scene following, in his famous account of how Desdemona fell in love with him by listening to his war stories, Othello says:

> This to hear
> Would Desdemona seriously incline:

But still the house affairs would draw her thence;
Which ever as she could with haste dispatch,
She'd come again, and with a greedy ear
Devour up my discourse. Which I observing,
Took once a pliant hour, and found good means
To draw from her a prayer of earnest heart
That I would all my pilgrimage dilate,
Whereof by parcels she had something heard,
But not intentively . . .

Incline is a lovely verb. It suggests the physical leaning of an awakened young woman, thirsting with her body as with her ears, as well as the sense of *being inclined,* of *having an inclination.* I like *greedy ear,* more commonplace to us because *greedy eyes* has become a cliché, but still very graphic. But how about *pliant hour?* That stops me each time. Again, it packs several possible meanings: *pliant,* in the sense that she would bend to his wishes, be *compliant,* and make herself available for an hour; *pliant* in the sense of *pliable,* with amorous implications physical and psychological; *pliant* in that the hour, time itself, could seem to stretch to accommodate them. These are small things, but they twinkle out of Shakespeare's language like stars: you see one, then another, and when you widen your gaze you see that his sky is ablaze.

I have the certain conviction that when we light on such a word with a twinge of pleasure, we are very close to the mysterious Shakespeare himself: his ghost sits with us. His genius, like Mozart's, may have gushed forth so plentifully that, as Ben Jonson remarked, he never erased a line. But even such profligate genius, scattering brilliance like a peasant broadcasting seeds, even his teeming brain must have felt an atom of pleasure as he wrote *greedy ear* and *pliant hour.*

Then there is another level of pleasure in the astonishing richness of metaphor. Several that come towards the end of *Othello,* as the sense of doom mounts, have played in my imagination since that first production at Dalhousie.

One is the moment when Iago drives Othello into a fit by goading him to believe that Desdemona is unfaithful with Cassio:

> By heaven, I would most gladly have forgot it:—
> Thou said'st,—O! it comes o'er my memory,
> As doth the raven o'er the infectious house,
> Boding to all . . .

What a stunning image for the sickening way dreaded thoughts continually pass and repass as shadows over distressed minds. It is made stronger by the verb *boding,* another strong Anglo-Saxon word, which Shakespeare lifts out of its more usual passive sense of something being an omen—by making it active; *boding to all* somehow implies a sound, the dry rasping cry of a raven on a winter afternoon. Macbeth says:

> The raven himself is hoarse
> That croaks the fatal entrance of Duncan
> Under my battlements.

There is Emilia's neat metaphor for Iago's suspicions of her:

> Some such squire he was
> That turn'd your wit the seamy side without,
> And made you to suspect me with the Moor.

The line is wonderfully in character for Emilia, both the clothing metaphor for a lady's maid and the characteristic tartness of her tongue when addressing her husband. It is a line that spits *t*s. It can be said with the teeth clamped in contempt. But consider also how economically it says so much.

Then, near the end of the play, the use of the candle and the rose as metaphors for mortality:

> Put out the light, and then—put out the light!
> If I quench thee, thou flaming minister,
> I can again thy former light restore,
> Should I repent me:—but once put out thy light,
> Thou cunning'st pattern of excelling nature,
> I know not where is that Promethean heat
> That can thy light relume. When I have pluck'd the rose,
> I cannot give it vital growth again,
> It needs must wither . . .

No high-flown flights of fancy for the prosaic soldier caught in this terrible web, but tangible everyday images. Their very homeliness makes him and us comprehend the enormity he is about to commit: to suffocate this woman we know to be innocent.

Othello also had a practical influence on my life. It introduced me to what became my profession—broadcasting. The night of the final performance, a tall, gaunt, well-tailored man with a black mustache came backstage to see me. He was Stephen Kerr Appleby, a producer for the CBC. He had liked my performance and asked whether I would be interested in doing some acting on the radio! Me, a freshman? Whom else had he asked? No one. The word got around quickly. The girl who played Desdemona, Willa Jean Seely, said generously to me, "I'm not surprised. It's obvious that you have talent." She was not burning with theatrical ambition herself and said it so unaffectedly I believed her. Hell, I would have believed her however she said it. Affectation didn't bother me then: I was up to my ears in it.

I was so thrilled I didn't want to talk about it very much. I went to the end-of-the-play party, which is always burdened with the intense longing not to let the experience and feeling evaporate, to postpone the return to humdrum life. Afterwards I went back to my room and lay on the bed to savour the news.

The CBC would *pay* me for acting: pay me, as short of money as I could be: I would be a *professional!*

Appleby followed up immediately. In those days the CBC broadcast a lot of "live" drama for the Atlantic provinces of Canada. They used a large studio on the top of the Nova Scotian Hotel. There was a small group of actors used regularly, like a repertory company, and I was drawn into the group. At first they used me in programs for schools. A few weeks after *Othello* I did *Treasure Island,* then *The Count of Monte Cristo* and *Kidnapped.*

I had nearly paralysing mike fright at the first broadcast. We stood at microphones, and when I stepped up to give my first line, the muscles in my calves began trembling so violently that I thought my legs would buckle. My hands holding the script shook and the only organ not seized up with terror was my voice. After that the fear went away, and ever since I have found it far more challenging to appear on a stage than to broadcast.

We were in the last days of live radio drama, using all the techniques that have since disappeared. In a glass-walled booth, a sound-effects man climbed steps, knocked on doors, walked on gravel, and produced the wind, the sea, or the cry of gulls on demand. But the actors contributed some of the effects as well. In *Monte Cristo,* we played the scenes in which the count is digging his way out of the dungeon with wastepaper baskets lying on music stands next to the microphones. To make the ambiance sound hollow, like a tunnel, we spoke our lines half into the wastebaskets. In *Treasure Island,* I was studying my part while others were rehearsing when the director, Appleby, asked through the loudspeaker, "What's that noise?" After some confusion, it turned out to be the squeaking I was making by rocking gently in an old wooden office chair. He asked me to go on making it while the sound man listened. They kept it in the broadcast with me, or someone else, creaking gently in the chair to simulate the rigging of the ship *Hispaniola* bending to the trade winds.

The sound effect that took more getting used to for a fellow of my small experience was kissing. I graduated with Appleby's group to adult plays broadcast in the evenings. In one I had to play a series of love scenes with a pretty actress called Miriam Newman, who was enough older, say twenty-nine to my nineteen, to make me feel a very raw youth. The sound of kissing was achieved by kissing one's own hand. We stood, man and woman, facing each other, a few inches apart, with a large microphone between us, each holding the script to one side of the mike, in order to get our mouths very close for the intimate, breathy parts. Miriam was extremely realistic, sighing and kissing the soft part of her right hand above the thumb until it was smeared with lipstick and, I thought, as a mere thumb, getting far too much attention.

They also gave me substitute work on a daily radio serial called *The Gillans,* in which I played a lazy farm lad who was always eating. Each of these broadcasts paid $5 to $15, depending on length. That sounds ridiculous today, but it was riches to me, at a time when my room and board cost $45 a month and tuition for an entire year at Dalhousie was $150. This was real money.

Appleby mounted the spring play for the Halifax Theatre Arts Guild with his usual group of players and gave me the juvenile lead in Samson Raphaelson's *Accent on Youth*. The next winter, the Guild entered it in the Dominion Drama Festival preliminaries for the maritime provinces and I won the best-actor award. I had also won an award for playing the flamboyant title role in the one-act play *Campbell of Kilmohr* in a competition at Dalhousie. So in May 1950, when I went off to fulfill my summer obligations to the Navy, I had a head full of theatrical ideas that had some realistic foundation.

Half the naval training was ashore, the cadets rising at six to double down to the harbour for boat pulling and doubling back up for hot cocoa and calisthenics, before a day of classes in everything from navigation to firefighting. The rest of the time we spent at sea, aboard a frigate, *La Hulloise*. I was put in charge of a watch, which theoretically augured well for the POC (power of command) and OLQs (officer-like qualities) needed for a naval career; but I was thoroughly bored most of the time, which did not.

I collected my summer pay in September and decided to stop playing with the Navy. My father was stunned, and a friend of his in Naval Intelligence, Commander Ted Watt, came to see me. A poet himself, he was very sympathetic to the creative temperament, but he had another mission. He asked a lot of questions about the other cadets, what they felt about the weekly parades, what we did, what the officers and instructors were like, and above all why I wanted to get out.

"Well, I'm really more interested in other things," I said, trying not to be rude about the Senior Service.

"Do you realise that is exactly what the Communists would like to have happen: to have young men like you quitting the service just now?" (The Korean War had begun that summer and Canada was involved.)

"Do you think you could help us out?"

"What do you mean?"

"We think there may be people who have deliberately infiltrated the UNTD to destroy morale, to discourage people like you, to encourage the idea that it is boring, that there's no point to it. If we could count on you to stay in, go to the parades, and keep your eyes and ears open, it would a great service for your country."

"Open for what?"

"Anything that makes you think someone is turning people away from the service. I'll be very honest with you, and this is highly confidential. We are having a lot of trouble with recruitment and with holding people—people like you."

He played on my vanity and my guilt about my father's ambitions for me. "Your father would be very proud of you if you could help your country—help us in this way. This isn't a game. This is deadly serious."

And he left me an out: "I'll make a deal with you. Stay in till next term. Go to the parades. Give me a report on anything you observe that discourages attendance, that makes the exercise seem boring or pointless. At the end of that time, if you still feel you want to get away to other things, I won't stand in your way."

Thus recruited as the humblest level of spy conceivable, but unable to take it all seriously, I attended a few more weekly parades and "kept my eyes open." I saw no conspiracy. It needed no red infiltrator to convince many of us that the evenings were tedious: an hour of drill in a dusty hall, lectures so elementary they were funny. I knew that the Navy and I had each been spared an inappropriate marriage. I quit, writing to the commander to explain, and to my father.

My letter brought the strongest blast I ever had from him. It made me heartsick to read it, but angry too, and all the more determined to go my own way. His letter was melodramatic. I had disgraced him and the service in which he had fought. He was ashamed that a son of his was "such a quitter." I was moved but not deterred.

In any case, if I was betraying him and my country, it was not to Communist agents; the true villain was William Shakespeare.

That addiction was deepened by a college production of *Romeo and Juliet* in which I played Mercutio and the small Apothecary part. The combination produced good notices and they were followed by the Dominion Drama Festival Award for *Accent on Youth*. My parents put aside their anguish and reacted generously when stories appeared in the Ottawa papers. The awards and reviews brought more radio parts from the CBC and welcome money.

Suddenly, however, the family had graver problems. At only forty-five, my father had a heart attack in Ottawa. It came so quickly after his violent emotional outburst about the Navy that I felt instantly guilty, assuming that my defiance had caused it. I thought a long time about what to write him. For once words were blunt tools. All the poetry I knew, all the Shakespeare sounded phoney and glib—literary emotions. For the first time in my life I needed to find words for my own real feelings, not the emotions of poets *recollected in tranquillity*. A feel for language was fine, but it did not easily translate into honest expression. Fine phrases reeked of affectation, insincerity. After a long struggle to discover how sincere I was, I found some very simple words of sympathy and confidence in his recovery.

That recovery became the family's main preoccupation and I was left to my own devices a thousand miles away in Halifax.

I virtually lived in the building that housed the Dalhousie Glee and Dramatic Society. I shared an attic room in an old house a few streets away, but gravitated to the Glee Club office every morning, as did several others. There we breakfasted on chocolate milk and cigarettes and rationalised not going to lectures. As often as not, I skipped them. I lived with a half-pleasurable ache of remorse for neglected studies, pleasure in my freedom, and longing to be in the theatre. I couldn't get enough of it. I spent most of the day time in that office.

My confidence was so unbridled that when the Arts and Science Society, the biggest student group, asked me to choose a play for inter-faculty competition, I managed—with a straight face—to persuade them to accept a play I had written. Of course with me playing the leading role, directing, and designing. And they agreed! It was awful—maudlin, juvenile, and largely incoherent—but it got on the boards. Modesty was not one of my problems.

The radio acting led to a job as a summer replacement announcer with the CBC. There was not a lot of work to do, but it was well paid and made me feel very much a working broadcaster. Not many network programs originated in Halifax, so the only announcements to make were brief continuity spots and station identification: "CBH, Halifax." The most senior announcers occasionally got to say, "This is the Trans-Canada Network of the Canadian Broadcasting Corporation." I practised mightily to be ready in case I ever had to say those weighty words, but it did not happen that summer.

That civilised interlude ended. I was quickly broke again,

so broke that I had to paint the outside of my landlady's Victorian house to catch up on twenty weeks of back rent. I loathed the idea of going back to college now that I had had a taste of work.

Nothing offered until late one night when the fellow who shared my attic came back from his job as a proof reader on the morning paper. Thomas Rogers was a young Englishman. We were not close friends but got along well enough to share our rather crude flat under the eaves lit by a semicircular window onto the street. The one thing we had in common was a belief that our lives were short on adventure. That morning he woke me up at four o'clock to show me a classified ad he had just proof read. It said two crew members were wanted on a schooner sailing to the Caribbean for the charter trade.

"Nobody else will know about this until the paper hits the streets. It gives us at least a three-hour head-start."

I didn't need to discuss what he meant. He meant adventure. He meant getting out of there, of his tedious job reading proofs half the night, and my hand-to-mouth existence as an actor. The previous day I had been reduced to cashing in all the milk bottles lying around for sixty-five cents to buy sweet potatoes to make dinner.

Rogers paid for a taxi down to the Royal Nova Scotia Yacht Squadron, off which the schooner was anchored. I had crewed out of there and knew where the dinghies were kept. We borrowed one and, with the dawn just touching the harbour, rowed out to hail her. She looked massive above us as we waited. The owner came on deck and invited us below. We talked in the handsome, panelled saloon for a long time. He was a friend of Errol Flynn's, he said, and intended to team up with Flynn's boat in the Caribbean for profit and adventure. I wondered a little about the nature of the adventure when he showed us, as though part of the ship's gear, a rack of many rifles behind the panelling. The upshot was that he engaged us for one dollar a month and all expenses until the chartering began to be profitable. Then we would get paid. It was a bargain to us. We shook hands, rowed ashore, and walked all the way back to Henry Street full of wild excitement. We had no doubts. This was it! We were off to see the world!

The sudden news floored my grandmother Daisy Oxner, who had the gravest misgivings. But I talked my way past them. We gave notice to our landlady, sold or gave away or boarded things like books with friends, and moved aboard the schooner.

Things did not happen as rapidly as the owner had promised. The experienced captain he kept referring to did not show up. We existed for two days exclusively on thin pancakes served with lemon juice and sugar. On the third day he took Rogers with him to the ship chandlers downtown, and, left alone on board, I began to look at the ship with less romantic eyes. Her standing rigging, the shrouds and stays that hold up the masts, looked very old and unreliable. Poking around in the forepeak, I found she had been holed at the waterline. The timbers had not been replaced, just covered with a metal sheet bolted on and painted.

When they got back aboard and the owner was busy, I passed on to Rogers my suspicion that the ship was not seaworthy. That and the owner's odd behaviour about food and so forth convinced us to get out. The next day we jumped ship, leaving the owner a note saying he could easily find others, since he had told us dozens had answered the ad.

Our landlady gave us the room back (no crowd waiting for that) and a telegram from my father. He had used the resources of the RCMP to check on the owner and advised me in the strongest terms to "stay clear of him."

A day or so later, someone told me there was a job going at a commercial radio station, CJCH. I applied and was hired as an all-night disc jockey. That was something quite foreign to what I did but it was a job.

I knew nothing about popular music or the world of the smooth-talking guys who purveyed it. I didn't know the patter that was in vogue for disc jockeys. But when I tried to borrow it from the other announcers, sentences like "Okay, guys and gals, here's a real purty toon" sounded ridiculous on my lips. I could not think of it as playing a part: I was acting in radio plays, and putting on different accents and personas was fun. This was different. I assumed that the announcer persona had to be the real me, as though the radio were a vigilant presence I couldn't lie to. So that's what the job got: the real, square, unhip me. I wasn't even at home with local popular slang, let alone the Southwestern drawl that was taking over the pop music scene even in Canada.

My background and interests had put me well out of the mainstream of popular culture, and my language showed it. I talked like a book. I was a kid who could read a line of Shakespeare quite easily, who wasn't at home with the common vernacular of his own time; or knew it to hear it but didn't speak it naturally. I didn't say, "Waddya mean?" but "What do you mean?" like a priggish elocution coach. I pronounced the *ings* and said *neither . . . nor,* and so on. It was as natural to me as wearing a jacket and tie all the time, something I had done at school since I was thirteen. Not to wear a tie in public places made me feel undressed, uncomfortable. So did dropping my gs. I had emerged from the factory of my education heavily starched. The disc-jockey job was just the first of a lot of launderings needed to loosen me up. I liked the formality, not realising how it probably grated on others, sounding condescending or *stuck up,* as a girl I dated told me—dated briefly!

At the radio station, feeling silly and awkward trying to play the flip disc jockey, I limited that role to my first hour or so, then gradually introduced what I liked. I played classical music, almost never heard on that station, and read poems. Occasionally it struck me that people forced to be awake in a seaport town all night—watchmen, guards, sailors and soldiers on duty, people in bakeries and factories—might not be thrilled to hear some kid with a plummy voice read poetry at three in the morning. Anyway, I did it, and when the phone rang while I was reading (presumably to protest) I ignored it. My selections were long ballads: "The Highwayman" by Alfred Noyes, Wilde's *The Ballad of Reading Gaol,* and shorter pieces like Harold Munro's "Milk for the Cat." I hesitated over Eliot's *The Waste Land,* because I was so besotted with it, but thought that would be pushing my luck with the radio audience. "The Highwayman" was perfect: easy to understand, a fine galloping rhythm, a lusty story packed with sensuous images.

I seem to remember there being requests for repeats. If not, perhaps I said there were to have an excuse to re-run the tapes. When I broadcast the poems for the first time, I recorded them so that I could replay them later and thus fill another half hour of tedium "in the dead vast and middle of the night."

One part of the radio job suited my rather formal way of speaking: the news. Every hour on the hour, there was a news bulletin to deliver. That meant reading a five-minute summary prepared by the British United Press radio wire. It is still known in the business as *rip and read* or *rip 'n' read*. If you forgot the time and neglected to rip off a fresh summary, you simply read the one from the hour before, with extra conviction.

I had been on the job only a few weeks, in late October, when one item leaped up at me from the 3 a.m. summary. The schooner we had briefly joined had foundered in a gale in the

Gulf Stream, a hundred miles off shore. Her masts had been carried away. She was leaking badly and was being towed back into Halifax. I read the item with a certain emotion. My fears about her seaworthiness had been right. The wrecked schooner eventually arrived in Halifax and spent the winter, forlorn and distressed, on a mooring in the Northwest Arm. You could see her from the Dalhousie campus when I visited there.

I did not miss college that winter. I was extremely busy. Several days a week I now had a permanent part in the radio serial *The Gillans*. When I got home from the all-night disc jockeying I would sleep for three hours, then go to the studio. There were other radio plays for the CBC in the evenings, and an actor returned from England, Peter Donkin, formed a new stage company. Our second production, *The Importance of Being Earnest*, with me as Algernon, was a finalist in the Dominion Drama Festival in St. John, New Brunswick.

Each of these exercises, and whatever applause they earned, fanned my theatrical ambitions. I suffered through the nights at CJCH, spending as much time as possible reading. So in a sense I continued my English major out of college, because I was reading, in new comprehensive Penguin editions, D. H. Lawrence, Evelyn Waugh, Aldous Huxley, Virginia Woolf, and others, often getting through one book a night.

Encouraged by a professor at Acadia University, I applied to an acting school attached to a stock company in Massachusetts. For a fee they offered a month's instruction and acting experience in a barn theatre at Priscilla Beach, ten miles south of Plymouth. After a month, some students might be chosen for their Equity group to run the rest of the summer. This seemed to be everything I wanted—travel, adventure, and escape from the all-night shift, which I had come to loathe, because I never got enough sleep. I would take catnaps during the night between records and got quite good at staying just enough awake to hear when the record needed changing. Sometimes I was too sleepy and missed it.

One morning, at the hour when tradition demanded country-and-Western music for early-rising farmers, I put on a record by Hank Snow, cued up another on the second turntable, and lay back as I often did to have a little snooze. Stretching out in the comfortable springback chair and putting my feet on the control console, I could get quite horizontal. This morning I drifted too far, because I awoke suddenly with a stab of fear, thinking I had missed the end of the disc. I hadn't, but I was so startled that in frustration I shouted to myself, "Jesus Christ. God damnit to hell!" and lay back feeling better. Then I noticed that the mike switch was on. Then the phone rang. There was only one call, an alert guy at the Canadian Press who kept me on all night and usually caught my flubs.

Spring came and I bought a car for $300 to be my transportation to the United States. It was a 1939 Hudson (this was 1952), and when I had had it for a week I heard about a man who had something that he wanted to get rid of, a 1934 SS-100, forerunner of the Jaguar. He had bought it in a neglected state and got it running again. I thought it looked incredible: a long hood, longer and more dramatic than its six cylinders called for; big chrome headlights, sweeping fenders, a cabriolet top, wire wheels, knock-off hubs—smashing. The owner wanted more conventional transportation for his family, so he took my '39 Hudson in exchange.

There was a lot of symbolism in this moment, a pattern to be repeated many times, as I struggled in the grip of inexorable double fate: a preference for things English and a passion for impractical cars. It did broaden my knowledge of the language. As in most technology postdating the Revolution, English and Americans developed parallel terminology, two different languages for automobiles, *cars*. The SS-100's long hood was a *bonnet* in England; the fenders, *wings;* headlights, *headlamps;* trunk, *boot;* windshield, *windscreen;* crank, *starting handle*— all of which vocabulary I had painful (and costly) cause to learn.

Innocently, however, I drove off, not south to the Spanish Main in a rickety schooner, but south to Broadway in my dashing car. I quit my job, boarded my books with a friend, said my goodbyes, and was off, with an immense feeling of freedom.

The trip was a series of small automotive disasters. Coming across the international bridge at Calais, Maine, the low-slung underbody hit a bump and punctured the gas (*petrol*) tank. I parked outside U.S. Immigration with the full tank gushing gasoline into the street. I asked the immigration officer if I might push the car to a service station next door and he refused to let me. When my formalities were completed I pushed the car with its tank now empty. Taking it off, welding the tear, and refilling greatly depleted my savings. I took off again, until somewhere in southern Maine the car stopped. So, expensive tow to a garage; expert diagnosis: generator not charging, car running on battery, battery flat. After a long battery charge, I drove on, afraid the damned thing wouldn't start each time I stopped. One more charge got me to the theatre at Priscilla Beach. The SS-100 retired to a daisy field.

The summer was better than I had hoped. I got parts of all kinds as a student and got taken into the professional company in August. My father and mother—he now recovered and somewhat reconciled to my ambitions—drove down from Ottawa with my brothers and rented a beach cottage. They came to see two plays and were generous about them. I had developed a somewhat convincing line in character parts but could also play straight juveniles and young leads.

That summer had quite an effect on the way I spoke. The first time I opened my mouth, someone laughed at my *ou* sound, the distinguishing Canadian diphthong that has special variations in Nova Scotia. I was saying *house* and *out* to rhyme with *hoase* and *oat,* both said very short. But there was a bubbly blonde from Louisiana who said *hey-owse* and made it sound like four syllables; another from Massachusetts who put *r*'s into words that didn't have them and dropped them from words that did. And someone from the Midwest who had vowels so nasal and flat you looked for the clothespin on his nose. I bristled a little at first: who was talking funny? But the instructor who had pointed it out was very helpful and said it was a professional handicap to saddle myself with so marked a speech difference. So I changed it, schooling myself to say *ow* instead of *owe*. Thirty-six years and a lot of professional speaking later, I am still insecure in the change and, when tired, lapse easily into the sound I grew up with.

When the summer ended, I was asked to join the permanent Boston Stock Company, to play at the Brattle Theater, Cambridge, that winter. We had started to rehearse the opening play, *Gaslight* (I was playing the Inspector), when the management announced that they did not have the funding to open. So we dispersed.

My beautiful SS-100 was a problem. Twice in the summer I had charged up the battery to take admirers (of the car) for a drive. Now she sat in the field, needing a new generator from England. I had no money. A mechanic offered me $65 for the car and I took it. My career was more important; I couldn't be saddled with material possessions. A dose of Zen that spring had left me feeling quite disconnected from objects, which merely shackled the spirit . . . so I told myself; but the SS-100 went with a pang. It is now a collector's item, worth something like $150,000. No matter: owning it those few months gave my spirits a great lift, and to drive out of Halifax in it, even if no one noticed, was worth $150,000—at least in Canadian dollars.

Several New York actors in the company gave me a lift to New York City. In the middle of the night I checked into a $5-a-night hotel on Lexington Avenue and began making the rounds the next morning. It was just after Labor Day and very hot. I cut a seedy figure, presenting myself at the offices of famous people like Guthrie McClintic, the late producer/director and Katharine Cornell's husband.

It dismayed me that his waiting room was jammed with actors who all looked nattier than Fred Astaire: tailored, creased, and shined. I had tweed jackets and a dark suit, all with traces of greasepaint from being used as summer costumes, scuffed shoes, and shaggy hair. But I got in where they were casting plays like *Billy Budd* and *Seagulls over Sorrento* and was interviewed civilly, if briefly. No, nothing just at the moment but please leave your name.

A well-off girlfriend fed me a couple of times and I went to the theatre once, to see Cronin and Tandy in *The Four Poster*. I was not thrilled by my first Broadway play and I got progressively less thrilled at keeping only grapes in the refrigerator in my hotel room, which was eating up my $65 very rapidly. After eight days, I was walking through Times Square to another appointment, feeling very hot, hungry, and sorry for myself, when a stern interior voice spoke to me. I stood still, on one of the islands in the middle of the roaring traffic, as the voice said:

"You're not meant to be an actor. You have some technique but you are too stiff, too contained, to be really good. You won't like this trailing around, sitting in offices with spruced-up Johnnies, selling yourself to get a part. It's too humiliating. You're meant to be a writer, not an actor—the cool one, behind the scenes. And if you're going to be a writer, you've got to go back to college!"

Nothing has ever been revealed to me with greater clarity, all at once. Usually career decisions make themselves slowly in some part of my unconscious and pop out, like a ticket from a parking lot machine, when needed.

I did what the voice told me. I borrowed the bus fare to Ottawa and moved in with my parents for a week. The next day I called on local radio stations and got hired by one.

My father's Depression conditioning showed that evening. When I told him I had got a job, he said, "That's great," and so on. We had a drink, and then dinner, and he kept coming back to it. After dinner, he brought it up again: "You got a job the first day you went out to look for one!" His voice had a quality I had never heard and I realised he was crying. He was embarrassed, but he couldn't stop himself.

"You went out and got a job—just like that? Do you realise how many years I walked the sidewalks, how many years I was out of work? You can't imagine what it was like."

Although recovered from his heart attack, he was pale and puffy, looking much older than his forty-six years. He was clearly aware of his own mortality and the limits on whatever dreams he still had. He had to take nitroglycerine pills to ease his angina pain. He was not supposed to smoke but still did, and still drank a little Scotch. The nitroglycerine pills thickened his speech. With two drinks and the pills, he could seem very drunk. He got maudlin and sentimental, as he often had in the past, but much faster.

"Jesus, and you go out—just like that—and they give you the first job you ask for."

"It wasn't the first. It was the second."

"It was the first day!"

"It's only forty-five dollars a week."

"It's a job!"

He had never shown me so much emotion before. The glimpse of his naked disappointments that evening, a sight of the wound the Depression had left; awareness of the limitations it had placed on him and the efforts he had made that I should have no limits, moved me. It made me feel adult, closer to him and a lot more tolerant.

CHAPTER SIX

I felt very close to their generation, people of my parents' age; young adults after World War I, marching in the army of the disillusioned. I had heard so much about it that I felt I knew their time as mine.

The First World War was a recent event, more recent in my childhood than Vietnam is today. It was called simply *the War*. Dad's father, though an American, had impulsively joined the Canadian cavalry at the age of forty. He knew horses. As a restless young man, stifled by his prep school in the East, he had spent time as a cowboy on a ranch in California. He was unlucky in Europe. His horse fell on him, sending him back a semi-invalid, even less competent a bread-winner than before.

Out of high school, so ripe for higher education, my father went to work as a teller in a bank. The family needed the money. A friend said he hated it: "He used to pace up and down inside the teller's cage in despair. He hated being inside and hated writing figures down in books."

The War was not only family stories, it was my reading. In the late 1940s and early '50s books about World War II were only beginning to appear. World War I and its aftermath were established literature. My sensibilities were shaped by people writing in the twenties and thirties. Perhaps it was merely being attracted to a set of emotions another generation felt intensely, but their time and their mood were congenial. The writer who best communicated it to me was T. S. Eliot, discovered in my second year at Dalhousie.

It was as though all the poetry stuffed into me had been in preparation for Eliot. In fact some of Eliot was an ironic collage of scraps from the literature I had been force-fed—and plenty I had never heard of. Eliot hit me like a sense of new possibilities on a clear morning with the sun trying to shine and the streets still wet from a night of rain. Eliot was London, the wider world, before I got there. I kept getting flashes of recognition but as a dream, "mixing memory and desire."

A large part of desire is memory and, just as a dream can imitate memory and stimulate desire, so did Eliot act on me.

> With the smell of hyacinths across the garden
> Recalling things that other people have desired.

He made me aware that you could be nostalgic for times that were never yours, you could vicariously feel experienced in things you had only read about. I kept meeting myself in Eliot.

Once, in the summer when I was ten, I fell hard while playing and hit my head on the ground. It half knocked me out, and in my ringing head was a quick movie of other children playing at the end of a short city street, a street where I had never been but knew very well. The light was golden and low, and their tinkling laughter had the echoes of summer twilight. On reading Eliot, I had the odd sensation of being in that street, that around the next corner those children would be playing. I can almost hear them behind his lines. There is an intense, aching familiarity which I can still conjure from "The Love Song of J. Alfred Prufrock":

Shall I say, I have gone at dusk through narrow streets
And watched the smoke that rises from the pipes
Of lonely men in shirt-sleeves, leaning out of windows?

It was as though Eliot were a short-wave radio broadcast
that I could receive on different frequencies, some better on
certain days than others.

There was the frequency of sexual imagery; very powerful,
understated images, capable of making even arms erotic:

And I have known the arms already, known them all—
Arms that are braceleted and white and bare
(But in the lamplight, downed with light brown hair!)

The sensuality, the calculating arousal of his symbols, coupled with the attenuated, world-weary attitudes, found mo-
mentary resonance in me. An anteroom of despair on the
threshold of life is commonly part of a young man's equipment,
and on first reading Eliot, I still carried the burden of virginity—
a disability that may now be as anachronistic as measles. Eliot
provided instant vicarious comfort for missed or fumbled opportunities; how much easier to *know* that experiences were
empty, to mask inexperience with a veil of indifference implying
too much experience. It felt smart to recite his parody of Oliver
Goldsmith in *The Waste Land,*

When lovely woman stoops to folly and
Paces about her room again, alone,
She smoothes her hair with automatic hand,
And puts a record on the gramophone.

I liked the Jazz Age flippancy of the image, the sudden descent
to the colloquial in the middle of more formal rhythms, but the

sentiment soon lost its piquancy. It did not fit our generation. Casual sex between *the young man carbuncular* and *the typist home at tea time* may have been symbolic of the arid, spiritually depleted world he was evoking. What seemed dry and pointless to him soon didn't to us. That world was not mine. There was a stage in which I read everything expecting to find the meaning of life on the next page, but a passing stage.

What never palled was the freshness of language and his power to provoke complicated associations from allusive fragments.

> I am moved by fancies that are curled
> Around these images, and cling:

What also delighted me was the fun in Eliot, the shafts of wit shooting through the elegies for lost faith. To one reared on music and verse of the nineteenth century and earlier, Eliot was as fresh as Gershwin: syncopated, iconoclastic, and satirical.

> O O O O that Shakespeherian Rag—
> It's so elegant
> So intelligent

Encountered in 1950, the poems still conveyed an irresistible sense of *now,* even though *now* was a quarter of a century old. Eliot made me feel worldly, travelled, and contemporary. And of course all this came down to words.

In any great poet the bonding of sound and sense is virtually unanalysable. As in living matter, the organic elements, broken down, mean nothing and I am not learned enough to unfuse Eliot's effects. What is evident to me is that his ear for the English language was perfect—the equivalent of perfect pitch—

for the harmonic range of our tongue, its rhythms, and all its voices—traditional and modern.

To this day, I make frequent therapeutic visits to his poetry, like an outpatient cured but returning for positive reinforcement. I visit for the pleasure of the language, a garden of simple blooms, as in "Portrait of a Lady," whose scents evoke worlds and worlds.

I return for the comforting sanity of words used in the right proportion, words he never has to reach for, everyday words given new grace, cleansed of extravagance.

> (where every word is at home,
> Taking its place to support the others,
> The word neither diffident nor ostentatious,
> An easy commerce of the old and the new,
> The common word exact without vulgarity,
> The formal word precise but not pedantic,
> The complete consort dancing together)
>
> —"Little Gidding"

In "Burnt Norton," Eliot complains that words "will not stay still," but his words do stay still. That is his genius. For me he is a standard of word weight, like the platinum bars kept in vaults to be the standard ounce or kilogram. That is why he is so refreshing to return to; his words do not "decay with imprecision."

After a week with my parents, I found a room of my own and enrolled in two night courses at Carleton College. The next year they gave me a bursary and I took a full credit load, mostly English courses. I began writing some verse, heavily imitative of Eliot, some criticism for the college newspaper, and a novel.

Living in the same town, but not at home for the first time, conferred new adult status, and my father and I found it a little easier to talk. Paralysed by the silence between generations, we had never talked. There were jokes, not conversations. In my teens, my mother kept urging him, sometimes in front of me, to tell me the facts of life. The nearest we ever got was after we had, embarrassingly, both witnessed a bull mount a cow on a farm we visited outside Ottawa. The next day, my father took me into town when he drove in to work. He brought the conversation around to the bull. I was fourteen, half embarrassed for me, half for him.

"You know what is fascinating?" he asked.

"No, what?"

"How wasteful nature is. The semen that bull put into that cow could make thousands of calves, but it all goes in one shot, millions of sperm, all spent in one shot."

"Yes," I agreed, wondering what was coming next, but nothing was. There was a long silence. That was my facts-of-life conversation from beginning to end. Later, I gathered under pressure from my mother, he gave me a book written in 1912. It urged tumescent young men to work off their "unwholesome urges" by "digging in the garden or going for a run." The advice came too late.

Ultimately he bridged this shyness with me by sharing his admiration for some of the earthier passages in literature. To make his teenage sons think he was one of the guys, he would throw out remarks like "He's as useless as a tit on a nun," with a glance to see if my mother had heard. He loved to quote Joyce's Private Carr from *Ulysses:* "I'll wring the neck of any bugger says a word against my fucking King." When he gave me a copy of *Ulysses,* he pointed out Molly Bloom's soliloquy, saying it was about as honest a piece of writing as there was.

After reading it, I didn't need any convincing. He did not take as enthusiastically to Henry Miller, when I was revelling in him a few years later.

He himself had a shy, charming way with women. I often observed him at parties, bowing, taking a woman's hand with the tips of his fingers; rather old fashioned, like the handkerchief he always kept in one jacket sleeve, as well as the one in his breast pocket. There was a little defensive distance in the perfect manners, but flirtatiousness too, especially with a much younger woman.

He had a strange pronunciation of the word *girl*. It came out *geer-rull*, half-swallowed, not the Scottish *gair-rul*, but an odd pronunciation like a note off key. It made me think that he had some hang-up about *geer-rulls* and, to my watchful adolescent eye, he behaved in their presence in a very self-conscious, smarmy way.

My mother suggested he had been no saint during the war and he let that implication hang around. Nostalgia for something explained the hours he spent listening to recordings of Ivor Novello's *The Dancing Years,* a hit musical he had seen several times in London in wartime. After the war, late at night, he would repair to those memories, a little tipsy and mawkish. Domestic cares, a mortgage, and a desk-bound job must have seemed a tedious sequel to the excitements of wartime. Peacetime didn't suit my father, my mother often said, and that was obvious.

He got all his books reunited and arranged in his study and spent many evenings making a wartime scrapbook. After that he looked like a man the first time they close the cell door, when he knows the sentence is real. For a while he made an effort to be the attentive father of teenage boys. He became avid for Ping-Pong and challenged us every evening. He listened to hockey games on the radio and asked dutifully about school. He and my mother took up skiing as something to do with us. He was more active than he had ever been. I didn't know until much later that he had had rheumatic fever as a boy and that his weakened heart kept him off sports in high school.

The heart attack left him sedentary again and full of regret. Things had not gone well financially. The beautiful house they strained to buy right after the war proved too much. They sold it for a smaller house but he could not climb stairs after his heart attack and they took an apartment.

Whatever their disappointments, they were unquestionably supportive parents. Anything we did well was praised—overpraised, I used to think. We just never talked easily.

Hemingway was the symbol of our stifled communication. My father liked Hemingway, as Ben Jonson said of Shakespeare, "on this side idolatry." He read and re-read him so often and praised him so extravagantly that I rejected him as a reflex. I ignored him until I saw the movie of *For Whom the Bell Tolls,* which sent me to the book for more detail on what brought Ingrid Bergman into the sleeping bag with Gary Cooper.

In my later teens Dad began asking me frequently whether I had read any more Hemingway, and when I said no, he would say, "Well, what's the matter with you?" and then pass it off with a favourite line, mock angry, with a little Irish accent: "The back o' me hand to you!"

Several times he pulled out a particular story, one of the Nick Adams stories, or "A Clean Well-Lighted Place," and read me a little, as if to say, "Don't you get it?" I took the book and read the stories but, perversely, was not moved to rave about them.

Then, smug from a course on the English novel and loaded

with E. M. Forster, Aldous Huxley, and Virginia Woolf, I told him I found Hemingway lacking in humanity and subtlety, or some such sweeping criticism, implying that I knew more about both literature and life than he. He could get quite angry: "Your taste is all in your mouth, for Christ's sake! You don't know what good writing is."

"Bobbie, don't talk to him that way," my mother said. She thought his infatuation with the irresponsible Hemingway was somehow a reproach to her—as it was, indirectly. Hemingway mocked him for being tied down, his writing ambitions abandoned, his share of adventure behind him. So we argued and I threw at him any criticism of Hemingway that I picked up: that he was sexually inhibited, had doubts about his masculinity, hated women . . . etc. all of which denigration drove my old man up the wall. The tone was lighthearted but the undercurrents were strong. I was provoking him; realising, but not wanting to realise, that Hemingway was his way of telling me about himself and his unsatisfied hungers.

Now, my not living at home somehow put that behind us. We found many tastes in common and I could accept his suggestions for reading. He never pushed any other author as aggressively as Hemingway, which made me less defensive. It was probably his fascination with the Spanish Civil War which opened up twentieth-century Europe for me. He told me several times that he really regretted not having been there; that he was chasing rum-runners when the moral struggle of the century was to be fighting fascism in Spain. I was very keen on Orwell but found the factions in *Homage to Catalonia* impossible to sort out. "Well, then, you should read *Man's Hope*," my father said, which introduced me to Malraux. He lent me the autobiography of Arthur Koestler, who was a Comintern agent in Spain. Koestler hypnotised me: he personified the currents of Europe—Jewish Hungarian, journalist in Berlin during the rise of Hitler, Moscow-trained agent who rejected communism, who wrote in German, French, and English. Koestler persuaded me that there was more to life than English literature: he pointed the way to Freud, Jung, Proust, Sartre, Gide, and Mann. Each of them was a world in himself and a world I thirsted to know.

It amazed me how I could live on this planet, co-exist for years with someone like Thomas Mann—and ignore him. Not wilfully ignore but remain in ignorance of, never quite bothering to pick him up. But once I did pick him up, the spark lit by whatever cause—the word of a friend, the enthusiasm of a professor, wanting to share something with a girl, an attractive cover in the book store—the light went on in that dark house and I could not imagine how I had lived without entering it before. Then I wanted to examine every room, missing nothing.

Yet, decades of reading later, many authors remain dark houses to me, houses I pass in ignorance, authors I am *meaning to* read. One that embarrasses me to admit to is William Faulkner. I have tried a little, but he has yet to get me to spend the night with him. Once I do, for some quirky reason, finding him in a country hotel on a rainy weekend, left in the pocket of an airline seat, I will ask myself yet again: "Idiot, why have you gone all these years without reading every word this guy wrote? Think of all the trash you've read, when you could have been reading this!"

Reading became a really heavy activity when I was fourteen, when I found an entire shelf of G. A. Henty's historical novels in the Ashbury library. The plots were formulas, the characters two-dimensional. The same deserving lad from humble origins wore a midshipman's jacket at the Battle of Trafalgar or a hussar's tunic at the Battle of Omdurman, but I devoured them. They became a drug. On a weekend I would make sure I had a fresh one to start, like a smoker afraid to run out. I wouldn't want to stop. I'd take a book to the bathroom and forget where I was until someone shouted at me or my rear end began to cramp. Lying on my bed and reading for hours, I ran the risk of getting routed out to do something "useful."

"Why don't you go and do something?" my mother would say.

"I *am* doing something. I'm reading."

"It isn't healthy just lying there with your nose in a book," she would say, just as she said to my father. Thus harassed, I would find places to read where I couldn't be found—in the attic, in the woods, and at night under the bedclothes with a flashlight.

Often there was another variation: "You'll never make something of yourself, you'll never amount to anything, if you don't get your nose out of a book!"

Quite understandably, she wanted to insulate us from the difficulties they had had. Hundreds of times over the years, in the long moments over dishes (a frequent opportunity for sermons, and reminiscences, which electric dishwashers have killed), or when I was reading in a room I had neglected to clean up, my mother exhorted me to do things to "make something" of myself . . . "to get on in life." Every child of Depression parents knew that advice better than his prayers.

I never persuaded her that reading was *doing* something—the same woman who had created this insatiable appetite for books by reading to me for countless hours before I could read myself.

Now, sitting in my room on O'Connor Street in Ottawa, surrounded by books, I did not have to explain. That was real freedom.

That room gave me enormous pleasure, the first place really my own. It was almost two rooms, at the front of the house, an entry way big enough to hold a chest of drawers, and the telephone, separated from the large bed–sitting room by an arched opening. The bed was the most comfortable place to read. Books overflowed the night table and were stacked on the floor around the head of the bed. I bought my first record player and listened obsessively to my few recordings: Beethoven's Hammerklavier Sonata, Grieg's A Minor Piano Concerto, and a concert by Horowitz, mostly Schubert. I did not entertain or eat there, apart from the occasional bottle of wine and some cheese. I listened to music, dabbled a little with paints, and read. I worked at the radio station and followed the courses at Carleton.

One course was memorable because the professor's enthusiasm was so infectious. It was a small seminar in Chaucer, given to four students by George Johnstone, a thin man with large eyes and a prominent adam's apple. A poet himself, he brought such a sense of fresh delight, such spontaneity to Chaucer, that I caught it like a virus. The principal works we had to study became a joy, particularly *Troilus and Criseyde*. Johnstone read aloud a lot and, with his accent in my ear, I read to myself. The delicacy, psychological subtlety, and atmosphere Chaucer managed within the disciplines of his verse form, and the sweetness of his expression, left a lasting impression. There is no more beguiling scene in English literature than when Pandarus at last insinuates the two lovers together in the night, with the heavy rain falling outside, adding to their intimacy.

What caught my imagination, because Johnstone stressed it,

was the word *daunger,* Chaucer's term for the demeanour of a
woman who is not available; her modesty, her reserve, trans-
lated today as aloofness, coldness, disdain.

Pandarus, encouraging Criseyde to be warmer to Troilus,
says:

> So lat youre *daunger* sucred ben a lite
> (Let your aloofness sweeten up a little)

and warns her that old age will break it down in the end:

> And elde daunteth *daunger* at the laste.

And when they are finally entwined in each other's arms—
as Chaucer describes it, like honeysuckle twisted about a tree—
he declares:

> Awey, thow foule *daunger* and thow feare,
> And lat hem in this hevene blisse dwelle,
> That is so heigh that al ne kan I telle!
> (Away with reserve and fear
> And let them dwell in this heavenly bliss
> That is greater than I can describe)

Chaucer's meaning suddenly hit me because I was having
direct experience of the ability of a woman to transmit recep-
tivity to advances or indifference, alternately, like an invisible
magnetic field force—suddenly on, suddenly off. It is a mechanism by which a woman restores her privacy and, in a sense,
restores innocence. Criseyde was a widow, yet projected the
aura of an innocent girl.

It intrigued me then and still does that, despite our abundance
of words to describe psychological states, we no longer have a

Robert MacNeil

term for this most common human experience, fundamental to relations between the sexes. *Daunger* survives only as an obsolete form of *danger* and, for the curious, in Chaucer.

The years at Carleton would have been worth it for that alone. Chaucer is not an author one cracks easily, without expert guidance and inspiration.

A year after I returned to Ottawa, life got very much better for my father and mother. The RCMP saw that this was not a finished man, promoted him to superintendent, and made him commanding officer of N Division, the training base outside Ottawa. He and my mother moved to a house on the base, where she was happy with dogs and a garden, and he began to ride for exercise. He was also appointed an aide de camp to the Governor General, Vincent Massey, and their social lives turned glittery. To add to their satisfactions, where I had failed, Hugh succeeded: he was accepted by the new tri-service military college and thereby launched on a naval career.

My father perfectly fitted the new job. He was a natural commanding officer, frequently commended while in the Navy for the condition of his ships and crews. He was also very keen on the ceremonial side of military life. He loved drill, uniforms, medals, brass bands, and all the spit and polish of formal occasions. With his dress scarlets for the RCMP or the best blues in the Navy, he was tireless at polishing and pressing and brushing. He didn't want an orderly to do it. Looking after the leather himself gave him satisfaction. He burnished his riding boots and Sam Browne belt, softening the new leather with saddlesoap and neat's-foot oil, then polishing until it shone like newly-opened chestnuts.

His figure carried a uniform well: slim, just over six feet tall, he stood to attention with a slight backward arch which made him look taller. He was the officer the Mounties chose to escort

182

My father, mother, and Michael in 1954

Harry Truman and Winston Churchill when they came to Ottawa in the late forties.

At home, as a joke, he was forever practising the slow march, thumbs rigidly down the seams of his trousers, one leg advanced stiffly, sliding the toe forward and bringing the other up to it smartly. Long after the war, it was a tic that seized him at odd moments. "This is how they do the slow march," and he would demonstrate, in whatever he was wearing, including pyjamas. I thought it was very boring and silly. How could a man so interested in music and literature behave so childishly? It embarrassed me. Of the things he deliberately taught me, I'd have to give slow marching 10, sex education 0.

That year I had another of those "my life won't be the same after this" moments—over Dylan Thomas.

It was a rainy spring afternoon in Ottawa and I was visiting an actress, Flo Fancott. I had drifted back into the Ottawa Little Theatre, free of the obligation to consider myself an actor, to direct one play and appear in two others. I had played with Flo in *Private Lives*. She put on the new recording of Thomas reading *A Child's Christmas in Wales* and a few poems. One of them is now very widely known but Thomas's own reading is still startling to those who have not heard his voice, with its extraordinary resonance and richness.

> Do not go gentle into that good night,
> Old age should burn and rave at close of day;
> Rage, rage against the dying of the light.

I listened as though my whole body were ears. I had never heard anything like this church organ of a voice, or such a tumble of wonderful words.

Dylan Thomas had been on the poetry course at Dalhousie two years earlier but had not registered with me. Now I felt, as Emily Dickinson said, "as if the top of my head were taken off." Something began to come together for me that had taken all the time from childhood to understand: it was the *sound* of English that moved me as much as the sense, perhaps more.

Perhaps I have never quite grown up and still want the magic of being read to as a child, because words heard still touch me more deeply than words printed. Or perhaps I am a throwback to the long oral tradition of our race, listening greedily, memorising easily. Perhaps it is an assertive Celtic gene that makes the music of words essential to me, enriching their meaning and quickening the appeal to my emotions,

> mixing
> Memory and desire, stirring
> Dull roots with spring rain.

Even re-reading something as familiar as those lines of Eliot, I have to translate them into sound, by speaking them aloud, or in my mind's ear. The sound of the words governs much of the pleasure in them.

I am a mover of lips and a public mumbler when reading words worth savouring. If I am to take them into my consciousness, have them move me, I must know what they sound like. Reading the Russian novels, I had to pause at each new character until the sound of his name was fixed in my ear. If I couldn't hear the name, the character couldn't move on the stage of my imagination.

We forget perhaps that human language is primarily speech. It has always been and it remains so. The very word *language* means tongue. The ability to read and write is, at the most, five thousand years old, while speech goes back hundreds of thousands, perhaps a million years, to the remotest origins of our species. So, the aural pathways to the mind—to say nothing of the heart—must be wondrously extensive. Like the streets in a big city, you have many ways to get there. By contrast, the neural pathways developed by reading are arguably less well established, like scarce roads in uninhabited country.

When an idea travels through the brain to become speech, the little excitement leaves a trace, as a pioneer in the virgin forest left traces so that others could follow. In the old usage of the word, *trace* meant a way followed, like the Natchez Trace, the Indian path that became a highway through Tennessee and Mississippi. Today *trace* has a related meaning in psychology: when a stimulus leaves a permanent effect on the psyche, an *engram* or *trace* that forms the basis of memory. Since all of us as infants, and most of us as adults, pass infinitely more time listening and speaking than reading and writing, my assumption is that the aural tracings have made better circuits and carry a stronger current to the emotions than the parallel circuits carrying the printed word. Speak to me and you will move me; write to me and I'll have to think about it.

Until I heard Dylan Thomas read aloud,

> Through throats where many rivers meet, the curlews cry,
> Under the conceiving moon, on the high chalk hill,
> And there this night I walk in the white giant's thigh
> Where barren as boulders women lie longing still
> To labour and love though they lay down long ago.

and had only read the poem, I had missed the sensual meanings and the old poetic devices carried by the sound; the flavour the language gave off, like the scent of flowers when the air is warmed.

You can read that poem flat, like a grocery list, but you would have to be perverse to do so. The language sings. The insistent alliteration, repetition of initial sounds, *through throats, curlews cry, barren as boulders,* is a throwback to Celtic poetry and obvious on one level. But the way they are woven through the stanza carries the effect well beyond the obvious— the number of *th* sounds, hard *c*'s, and the richness of *l* sounds in *lie longing still/To labour and love though they lay down long ago* give a texture to the sound that is hard to describe but obvious to the ear.

Beyond the alliteration is the extraordinary rhythm created by the six-foot line and the word choice within it. Reading it aloud is the only way to feel it.

The meaning is not intellectually profound—the themes are sex, birth, death, decay—but there is something so vital and seductive in the uttering that the poems carry enormous conviction. Even when the torrent of words and images seems to obscure any meaning, meaning comes through. They seem chaotic but they are very carefully crafted. Thomas said he wrote "for the love of Man and in praise of God." That and the abundance of imagery from nature and the odd rhythms remind me of another favourite, Gerard Manley Hopkins:

> Nothing is so beautiful as spring—
> When weeds, in wheels, shoot long and lovely and lush;
> Thrush's eggs look little low heavens, and thrush
> Through the echoing timber does so rinse and wring
> The ear, it strikes like lightning to hear him sing.

Unless we *hear* such language we will have no ear for it. To *rinse and wring/The ear,* a habit of listening to words has to be cultivated and it is best cultivated young.

It is like music. By hearing you build up the layers of memory that create a critical ear. Spoken words clearly form the earliest layers because children live in the oral tradition. But even for the literate adult, undervaluing the importance of the sound of our language may shrivel the language sense.

Thomas moved into my imagination on two levels. The poetry gave me a wonderful sense of letting go with words, of abandon. As Virginia Woolf said of the word-coining genius of the Elizabethans, it was "as if thought plunged into a sea of words and came up dripping." Thomas made hearing words an aesthetic experience like music; the sound uppermost, as if his words spun a giant spider's web which the poet strummed, making you vibrate in sympathy.

The other Thomas, of the play *Under Milk Wood* and the prose, was a different man, irreverent and very funny. He became a symbol of freedom to me. He was the first living writer with whom I knowingly connected. His life seemed a paradigm for mine. His escape to London from crushing Welsh provincialism, fictionalized in *Adventures in the Skin Trade,* became a metaphor for my own need to escape from Canada. The Swansea he grew up in could have been Halifax or Ottawa, poetic in retrospect, stifling to the young imagination. Escape for him meant escape to London, as it did for me. London was his mecca—and mine. I devoured his account of arriving in London, letting fate take him, his finger stuck in the beer bottle, his encounters with sex and pretension. I had already longed to be there and he made the longing sharper.

His bawdy humour and earthy preoccupations delighted me, fitted my own view of life, and made Ottawa seem all the more staid. The poet Roy Campbell had come to Ottawa to lecture; why not Thomas? I imagined Dylan Thomas caught in Ottawa in midwinter, a dark Northern city where the pubs were not the convivial, cosy places in England but wretched, forlorn establishments of spilt beer and Formica tables; places for getting drunk and morose, or drunk and belligerent.

I imagined Thomas, with a belly full of beer and a bursting bladder, out in the black, brittle night, 25° below zero, when the insides of your nostrils freeze together as you breathe. There were no public lavatories. You were supposed to do that inside somewhere. Would he lean into a snowbank to pee, I wondered, as I did? Would there be a frozen yellow hole signed Dylan Thomas? Would it become a collector's item?

It had happened to me and Peter Hopwood, another student with writing ambitions. A few times he and I drank a lot of beer in one of the unattractive pubs, then repaired to the radio station where I worked to listen to Beethoven. We could never hear him loud enough anywhere else. CFRA was off the air on Sunday nights, but I had a key. We would go into the master control room, which had the biggest speakers, fire it up, and put on the Fifth Symphony or the Emperor Concerto full blast, then bathe in the sound.

One night, painfully full of beer, I couldn't find my key and we couldn't get in. We had to relieve ourselves against the outside wall of the building. For the rest of the winter, it never thawed and two yellow icicles stood reproachfully against the wall. They symbolised to me why Dylan Thomas should never come to Ottawa.

I was reading everything I could find about him, toying with the idea of staying in college after my degree to do a study of Thomas, perhaps a biography, when he died on his fourth, alcoholic visit to the United States. He was thirty-nine. Somehow, with the knowledge of his death, my ardour to study him evaporated; perhaps it was the scathing way he described young academics in "A Visit to America":

an earnest crew-cut platoon of giant collegiates, all chasing
the butterfly culture with net, note-book, poison-bottle, pin,
and label, each with at least thirty-six terribly white teeth.

My need to get away was stronger and I could pay homage to
him in London.

I had a third reason to identify with Thomas. He was the
first poet who fully exploited the possibilities of radio. His dazzling play *Under Milk Wood* and many of his stories were
written to be broadcast and his poems attracted a wider public
when he read them on the BBC. Indeed, one of his producers,
Aneirin Talfan Davies, believed that the radio influenced both
the audience and the poet: it drew people who "needed the
persuasion of the poet's own interpretation," and it caused
Thomas to strive "towards greater clarity and directness."

Radio was the medium most congenial to me, at first instinc-
tively and by the accident of being offered work, later for reasons I could analyse, among them being Canadian and born
into the radio age.

CHAPTER SEVEN

*T*he first radio broadcast I remember hearing was in 1936, when Edward VIII abdicated to marry Mrs. Simpson. The crisis roused us in a grey December dawn to listen in our pyjamas. My father must have had a few days ashore. I was nearly six. The day of the abdication was December 10, my brother Hugh's second birthday. The next day, Edward broadcast his explanation and left England. Listening to him, my parents stared at the radio, shaped like a gothic arch. They were hushed by the gravity of the event, the communications miracle that brought it to us, and the sense that the ordered world was coming apart.

Edward's voice, sing-song voice, saying:

> . . . I have found it impossible to carry the heavy burden of responsibility and to discharge my duties as King as I would wish to do without the help and support of the woman I love . . .

came to us in that strange filtered short-wave sound that became the background to all the years of drama ahead. Sometimes hollow, sometimes pinched and thin, against a hiss of atmospheric static and tuning squeals, the voices sounded as though they were churning across the Atlantic underwater.

The abdication gave the new broadcasting age its first global sensation. They came frequently after that.

Through that same attenuated sound we heard the wartime voice of Churchill, and at Christmas everyone stopped eating turkey and plum pudding to listen to the hesitant tones of the new King, George, trying to control his stammer. My mother always defended him hotly against any criticism of his speech difficulties: "He does very well, poor man. He never thought he would have to take on this terrible burden."

When the world really came apart in 1939, the crisp tones of those disembodied British voices carried a special authority. They touched us three thousand miles away with the wand of Empire, with majesty and dignity, a rightness that did not need to shout about itself. It was like the voice of God—as God was all wisdom and the fount of all knowledge—and naturally spoke with an upper-class English accent. God never spoke to me. The BBC did.

Although we heard many American entertainment shows, our radio war was British; not Edward R. Murrow, but the BBC. First, the chimes of Big Ben roiling through the distortions of the shortwave; then the voices, which I can hear now as if a record were playing.

> This is London calling North America. Here is the news, read by Derek Prentice.

They had a kind of power different from the television journalists of today because they dealt in words only. Nothing distracted the listener's attention from their voices and the words they spoke. They had no faces; they showed no pictures, and there were few sound effects. They did have names, but were otherwise anonymous. The very lack of more positive identity, the absence of personality, carried power, because the emptier their identities, the more abstract their voices, the more the audience fastened on to the words. The power was in the words.

What wisps of identity filtered through their measured delivery were freighted with all the more meaning. That they were British, and spoke with a particular British accent, helped to give Britishness and that accent enormous prestige around the world—in German-occupied lands and elsewhere, but especially in the British Empire. It is ironic that so potent a tool of imperial communications really emerged just as the Empire was about to break up. In Canada, as elsewhere, the voice of the BBC was the voice of sanity, civilization, and truth. If the King himself had read the newscasts they could not have had greater authority: the announcers were better readers.

As a child I didn't *listen* to the news, I *heard* it as background to what else was happening, the way I heard the Metropolitan Opera broadcasts on Saturday afternoons if I passed through the living room, without paying attention. I *listened* to other programs.

I learned my first singing commercial at seven in 1938, on a program sponsored by Sweet Caporal cigarettes:

> Light up and listen,
> There's music in the air
> Let your dreams float away on a song.

In memory, my father poses for me, as for an advertisement of that day, in a large easy chair, his sharp profile raised, his Sweet Caporal in one hand, the smoke rising serenely, while I sit on the floor listening. There is an actual cigarette advertisement that looks very much like him.

In that same year the radio created enormous excitement for me with the Jimmy Dale Club for young aviators. You could become a member if you sent two cereal boxtops, and members got a pair of *Silver Wings!* The words *silver wings* repeated many times created the strongest longing I had ever felt. To apply I had to fill out a form and answer questions. I did so as though my life depended on it, sprawled on the living-room floor, asking my parents what I should say. When the letter was posted, I have never waited for anything as eagerly as the reply. The wings came. Breathless with joy, I opened the envelope and found them. I wore them all the time, transferring them as I changed clothes. It was mid-winter and I put them on my coat to go outside. The wings were lost while I was playing in a big snowbank. I searched and searched, digging in the snow, shovelling it away, but could not find the silver wings. For as long as a child can be, over such things, I was heartbroken.

The voices on the radio had created a magical value for that piece of cheap, stamped metal. Any present I was given, even in those lean times, had far more intrinsic worth. It was my first brush with the power of broadcasting to play upon our fantasies, our covetousness, our fears. That was the year Orson Welles broadcast *The War of the Worlds,* convincing terrified America that Martians had invaded.

At first, radio was a controlled substance:

"Oh, please, just five more minutes."

"No, dear, seven o'clock is your bedtime and it's already a quarter past."

"Oh, please, just till the end of this program?"

With the war, and my father away, the rules gradually eased, and by the early forties I was soaking up *The Green Hornet, The Lone Ranger, Amos 'n' Andy, Fibber McGee and Molly, The Shadow,* and *The Lux Radio Theater*.

On days when I was ill and stayed home from school, there was an all-day feast, starting with *The Breakfast Club*.

> Good morning, good morning,
> It's time to get a lift,
> With a guy named Don McNeill
> And food products made by Swift.

If I was ill, but well enough to want to listen to the radio, I was usually on the living-room sofa with pillow and blankets. There was only one radio, a Philco with a racy twentieth-century streamlined look, too big to move into the bedroom.

At lunchtime there was a Canadian variety show called *The Happy Gang:*

> If you're happy and healthy
> To heck with being wealthy
> So be happy with the Happy Gang!

followed by the Dominion Observatory official time signal, then the BBC news. Then soap operas; wholesome and innocent Canadian dramas first: *Lucy Linton's Stories from Life;* then the racier, spicier product from New York: *Pepper Young's Family, The Guiding Light, Ma Perkins,* and *Young Widder Brown.* Can a woman who has once loved completely ever find true love again? the announcer asked urgently every day: pretty boring to a boy of ten or eleven. But his voice registered with me. Dipped in hot marshmallow, it sounded, coated with syrupy organ music, making the words *Procter and Gamble Hour* sound like something soft and furry you could curl up in.

Late in the afternoon, Canadian culture staged a quaint counter attack with *Don Messer and His Islanders,* old-time country music from Prince Edward Island. Then, just after supper, America reinvaded and occupied Canadian airspace until my bedtime with *The Green Hornet* and all the others.

There were Canadian programs—intrepid Mounties on endless dogsled missions in the North; a war series called "*L for*

Lankee" about Lancaster bombers—but they lacked the seductive American pizzazz.

One Canadian program, however, made the magic of radio personal to me. In the winter of 1943–44, my mother went out one evening a week to some gathering of other naval wives, leaving me in charge of my brothers. I was expected to go to bed at eight but secretly stayed up till nine to listen to a weekly serial called *The House on the Hill,* a CBC production in which a nice young couple called John and Judy got on with their lives together in a sentimental but lighthearted fashion. Doubtless they intended to comfort many war-severed families by their very ordinariness.

Their story drew me intimately into their affairs. Judy's voice had qualities—the hint of a chuckle, a musical timbre—that thrilled me. I was in love with her disembodied voice. Sneaking my weekly hour with her was my private vice. It was too early for anything explicitly sexual, but it was charged with promise, and I fantasised about her—not the actress, but the character.

I thought John was a namby-pamby jerk, obviously because I was jealous of all the attention, and affection, he got from Judy. I half convinced myself that she thought so too. He had one of those goody-goody CBC voices: produced in the back of the throat, full of integrity and clean living—the kind of voice a soft Mountie should have.

It is remarkable how much a voice on the radio conveys to a listener tuned to the right psychological wavelength. I longed to be in that imaginary house on the hill, so that I could listen to Judy all the time. I invested her with all sorts of desirable characteristics: a sense of humour, a willingness to make light of little things that didn't matter, a touch of little-girl playfulness. I made her a good sport, adventurous, and willing to go anywhere, while warmly affectionate and caring. I cannot remember a single episode or specific incident in the series, but the fantasy girl I created around her voice is very clear in my memory. No television program has ever involved me so personally. Partly it was my age, twelve to thirteen, but there was something else.

When I was alone listening to the radio, I was *alone* with it; it spoke particularly to me and I did not have the feeling that other people were listening. I seemed to be listening as privately as I read a book, reading to myself; I was *listening to myself*, in effect. Television gives me the feeling that other people are watching; even if I am alone, I cannot *watch to myself*.

It is a great pity that radio is so under-utilised in the United States. It is the thinking man's electronic medium and it is the broadcast medium for words. Radio could rehabilitate the use of words in a culture increasingly drugged by pictures; a culture in danger of losing the discipline and precision of linear thinking in a blur of mosaic impressionism.

For my generation, radio in effect re-created the aural tradition so rich in our Celtic-Gaelic past. Listening to the radio was like being told stories; we listened with the intensity of the people who listened for thousands of years in all cultures to the shaman, the bard, the story-teller, the minstrel, who embodied their history, philosophy, literature, drama, and the meaning of life.

Once, in the west of Ireland, I was taken to a pub after hours. My companion knew the landlord and we were let in to the bar room which seemed pitch black. The only illumination was a low peat fire. We were guided to a bench and given a drink, thinking we were the only customers in the place. But as our eyes gradually adjusted to the light and our ears to small sounds of human presence, we realised the room was full. With our arrival settled, they began quietly talking, singing songs and telling stories in the dark, the atmosphere perfumed by the peat and tobacco smoke and the fresh draught Guinness. There were only shadows to see and only voices and words to listen to. The reduced light, heightened concentration, sense of intimacy with the speakers, all evoked the trance-like mood in which I listened to radio as a child. The people listened—really listened.

There is something in radio appropriate to the Canadian spirit. Canadians envy American materialism, yet stand a little aloof and critical. Less sure of their nationhood, Canadians have less need to parade their patriotism, less need for the national rituals that Americans crave; they are more individualistic and more private, and radio is a private medium.

To be sure, television quickly became the dominant medium, but for historical and cultural reasons, radio meant more to Canada. It was the glue of modern Canadian feeling. Radio has held the nation together, while television is the medium of dissolution, of cultural absorption by the United States. In spite of laws requiring Canadian content, American programs dominate Canadian screens. Canadians watch American but listen Canadian.

For my generation, CBC Radio was the principal patron of Canadian drama, short stories, poetry, acting, and music. Today the CBC is still a model for the thoughtful use of the radio medium. On independent stations, the commercial possibilities are exploited as crassly as they are south of the border. On the CBC, the radio is proof of a different Canadian aesthetic.

I was clearly fascinated by radio. The summer I was ten, I took a large cardboard carton and made a shortwave radio set by drawing dials and gauges and switches all over the face. I spent hours playing at transmitting and receiving imaginary broadcasts, mostly to planes and ships.

I made my radio debut about that time as part of the war effort. Someone got the idea that British children, with so much to endure, needed cheering up by their colonial cousins. Four of us, Wolf Cubs, went to the CBC studios in Halifax, stood around a floor microphone, and sang songs to put heart into British Scouts far away. Our high voices sounded very thin and bloodless in the big studio as we sang:

> Put another little log upon the camp fire,
> Put another little log upon the fire . . .

and other stirring numbers. How could Hitler cope with a weapon like that?

Ten years later I was back in those studios acting for the CBC and for a summer of announcing. That was followed by nine months as the all-night disc jockey at CJCH, Halifax.

Now, in the fall of 1952, I had a job at CFRA, Ottawa, to support myself at college. Actually I had several jobs.

Their immediate need was for an announcer on the Sunday evening gesture to classical music called *Symphony Hall,* and when they heard the way I spoke they thought of classical music. So I did that. To fill up forty hours of work and justify my $45 a week, I was also control-room operator for afternoon programs. That meant playing the records and controlling microphones for the disc jockeys, something I had done for myself on the all-night shift in Halifax. On Saturday nights, I spelled the all-night disc jockey, John Corrigan, and had to dust off my pop-music patter. He called himself "Long John Corrigan" and specialised in country-and-western music, with a religious sub-specialty. Around dawn he conducted a devotional hour he called *The Little Church in the Wild Wood* and his fans missed it mightily when he wasn't there. Since I was doing the program only one night a week, I was excused. I was out of training for the graveyard shift; it was hard to stay awake. I passed a lot of hours during LP records reading and typing up notes from college lectures.

After six months they took me off the control panel and put me in the newsroom, so I had my first taste of journalism. CFRA was one of the first commercial radio stations with a professional newsroom, and it covered the Canadian capital responsibly. I helped to write and edit copy for the news announcers to read on the air.

It was my first real immersion in journalese and I brought an academic squeamishness to the driving style that felt as utilitarian as freshly-poured concrete. Later, as a wire service man myself, I came to admire its utility and, in good hands, its grace.

After I had been at CFRA for a year and a half, there was an opening at the CBC for a staff announcer and I got the job. The CBC was a large organisation and to join it was a little like joining the government—a lot of rules and restrictions but infinite security. People stayed for life. At first the job was perfect for someone as busy as I was outside, studying, writing, working in the Little Theatre.

The duty announcers worked in shifts and, since Ottawa originated few national programs, there was little announcing actually to do. We sat in a comfortable, quiet studio, waiting for the half-hour break to identify the station and make short announcements about upcoming programs—rarely more than twenty seconds in all. Waiting to do only that could make some announcers very nervous; after years of it, some still glanced constantly at the clock and coughed anxiously to be sure their throats were clear when the moment came.

There was no need to listen to the programming in between, so I read, wrote, or day-dreamed. It was very easy work, well paid, with good benefits. I felt I was gradually falling asleep for ever.

I had always assumed that the word *announcer* was a term invented for radio, but the *OED* shows the verb *to announce* (from French and Latin), meaning to *make known* or *to deliver news,* appearing in Caxton in 1485. I suppose the most celebrated *announcer* ever was the Archangel Gabriel, who gave Mary the message that she was to conceive a son, yet remain a virgin. He delivered this improbable news so convincingly that they named the event after his job, *The Annunciation,* and for hundreds of years the best artists of the time painted it. That left *announcing* a lot to live up to, but, in 1955, the inspiration was made explicit: Pope Pius XII actually made Gabriel the patron saint of people in radio, television, and other electronic communications.

The announcer function is first defined in Cotgrave's dictionary of English and French in 1611:

> *Annonceur,* An announcer, declarer, proclaimer, signifier, advertiser

—all of which sound pretty familiar to us.

In 1802, Smollett, translating *Gil Blas* from the French, said: "The announcer is a domestic who stands in the hall on visiting days and pronounces aloud the names of the company as they come in."

It is hard today to think so condescendingly of *announcers,* so grand has broadcasting made the function, and so central to our culture. They are now famous and well paid, fawned over and sought after as celebrities for their ability to read convincingly what someone else has written. They are more celebrated than what they say. As individuals they become powerful and their celebrity becomes a commodity. And if they have not yet presumed to the heights of the Angel Gabriel, one, with a detour through Hollywood and California politics, has at least become President of the United States.

Broadcasting made people powerful because its technology carried their voices to millions of ears. The voice that touched five thousand ears from a small, low-power radio station in Kansas had five thousand times the power of the voice that talked to one person over the fence, although what it said did not have to make any more sense. The voice emanating from New York City and reaching ten million ears and minds had correspondingly more power. Those millions did not ask whether the thoughts the announcers intoned so movingly, so importantly, were their own thoughts, the words their words, whether they were clever or stupid, learned or ignorant. The millions, sophisticates and innocents alike, took those voice-personalities into their imaginations and wove out of those tendrils of sound a fabric that clothed a different Americanism; cloaked them all in a new feeling of oneness and togetherness. The farmer in Iowa, the Wall Street broker, the Detroit autoworker, had the same Fibber McGee joke on their lips, the same singing commercials in their heads, when they met their fellow Americans the next morning.

Those programs had equally devoted followings in Canada, and so did American television when it arrived. Shortly after I got to the CBC as a radio announcer, they opened the first television station and I became one of its announcers. The station was bilingual, the Ottawa-Hull area having more French- than English-speaking residents, so there were two announcers in theory, often just one in practice, who had to make do in the other language. I often had the duty of regaling French listeners with this sign-off:

Et, maintenant, avec l'audition de *God Save the Queen,* nous vous disons—bonsoir.

The television station soon got a mobile unit and used me as announcer, or presenter, on its first broadcasts originating outside the studio. The first one might well have ended my career before it started.

Every summer the capital boasted the Ottawa Valley Exhibition, rather like a state fair. This year the CBC televised it for the first time—live. The opening found me standing with the director of the "Ex" and his assistant and holding a lollipop mike. I said something like:

> Good evening and welcome to the first television broadcast from the historic Ottawa Valley Exhibition. Before seeing the sights of this year's "Ex," we are fortunate to have with us the man who has has made this Exhibition one of the leading events of this region for the past twenty-seven years, the director, Mr.— I'm terribly sorry but I seem to have forgotten your name.

He told me and I started interviewing him. A few seconds into the interview, I realised that I had also forgotten the name of his colleague, who was standing on my other side. In a few moments I would have to turn to him. I kept prolonging the first interview, barely listening to the answers, while I tried to think of the second man's name. It wouldn't come. The floor manager was waving at me to move to the other man, so there was nothing to do but thank the director, turn to the other man, and say, "You're not going to believe this, but I've forgotten your name too!" He believed it and didn't look too happy about it.

Incredibly, they gave me more assignments, like live broadcast coverage of the arrival of the Duke of Edinburgh at Ottawa airport. The entire Canadian Cabinet went out to greet him. Deep in the bowels of the broadcast truck I was to do a commentary, identifying each person who shook hands with the Duke. Innocent of politics, my mind on the higher things of life, I knew very few of the ministers on sight. I made a file card, with each name and title on it, arranged in the order they were to be presented. Pierre Normandin, the producer, who was standing with his head through a hatch in the truck, agreed to hand me a card as each minister shook hands. The system was not foolproof. By the time he saw the person, leaned down, and reached out his arm, that man had gone and the next picture was up. We were wrong with every one, only one man wrong each time, but that is as wrong as you need to be. The program was shown across Canada.

Nevertheless, they gave me a weekly program entitled *Let's Go to the Museum,* designed for children. At the National Museum of Canada, I interviewed experts on Indians, Eskimos, archaeology, pre-Columbian culture, and so on, with several bright children as foils.

I enjoyed it for twenty-six weeks; then it was the spring of 1955, and the task I had set myself, to get a B.A., was complete.

I was in love with a wonderful girl, and we planned to be married when she finished college the next year. I had a novel and a play in the works, and $2,000 in savings.

April was not cruel that year. As the ice broke up on the Ottawa River, it was not Eliot's spirit in my blood but Chaucer's, because the time had come to go on my long-awaited pilgrimage.

When I quit my job at the CBC, they told me very nicely, "You're not smart to give up this job. You could make a very good career. Why don't you take a leave of absence?" I thanked them politely, holding back any desire to say that I could not spend my life there introducing the Dominion Observatory official time signal. When I told them at the television station I was leaving, they said similar things. Nothing would have kept me. If they had offered to double, triple my salary, it would not have tempted me.

I felt like Joyce escaping from Dublin at the end of the *Portrait of the Artist as a Young Man,* not quite pretentious enough to say it to others, but shouting it silently to myself: "I go to forge in the smithy of my soul the uncreated conscience of my race," or something like that.

I had to go to England, where I thought all the words came from. I thought I could do anything.

CHAPTER EIGHT

꿎

*M*y father still had itchy feet. Eighteen months after
I left Ottawa, he retired from the RCMP at fifty,
joined Canada's Department of External Affairs,
and moved my mother and Michael to London, too. Since Hugh
was now a midshipman in the Navy, studying at Greenwich,
the whole family was in Britain.

My father's job was to supervise security in Canadian em-
bassies, which meant doing what he had wanted to do all his
life—travelling extensively in Europe. Such strenuous activity
was a bad gamble with his heart condition, but he knew that
perfectly well. He told me about it in the most open conversation
we ever had.

It was a summer evening in London in 1957 and we were
alone in their flat in Portman Square, with a view eastwards
over the rooftops to Broadcasting House in Portland Place. I
was staying there to be near the hospital where my wife had
given birth to our first child, his first grandchild, a few days
before. The outside light was dying and we did not turn on any
lamps.

My mother was very worried about him because he would
not discuss his condition with her. She said he had never wholly

207

confided in her. He would not tell her who his doctor was; she was not totally sure he had one.

He must have been aware that I had been watching his behaviour because he wanted to explain it. He still took nitro-glycerine pills, but secretively, and the previous evening I had noticed their effect, wondering whether he was still drinking as well.

He appeared tired; then his speech thickened; then the quality of his thought deteriorated, as though his brain were slowing down. His vocabulary shrank; his body was tense with the effort of concentration. His mind would fix on a trivial point, and his conversation would go around and around it. His eyes looked glassy, his mouth worked drily, and he smoked ceaselessly. He would begin a habitual gesture but form it grossly, his fingers trailing limply, without control. He would repeat a certain few sentences, then just one sentence, then a few words, until he was mumbling with a dull look in his eyes, his head loose on his neck, his body slumped in the armchair.

Yet through all this I could see the inner man fighting to resist. He told me he could see himself degenerate and was embarrassed that his family had to witness it, but he knew no other way of relief.

He said his condition was not good. There was a long silence in the dusk and then he said he was worried because it was getting worse. One of the main coronary arteries was blocked and the others were hardened and therefore at risk. When he was tired or under strain or excited, the pain of the angina was intense, with a feeling that his chest cavity was being crushed from the front and back. He said the pain was frightening and unbearable. When he took one of his larger pills to ease it, the effect was like that of drinking a tumbler of brandy quickly.

He was very worried but said he did not want my mother

My mother and father in London, 1959,
the year he died

to know. The job was much harder than he had expected and he did not know how long he could last in it. He thought he had three or four years at the most. I told him he should retire immediately and prolong his life. Several times he had mentioned a "cottage in Cornwall," in which they could live on his pension from the RCMP. I urged him to pursue that. No, he said, it wouldn't be worth it. It would add two years to his life at the most.

Several things were struggling in him. He was a sentimental man. The pathos of his situation moved him, yet I suspected that the idea of pushing it to the end had appeal, when he knew it would happen sooner or later. He loved going to new places. He hadn't lost that. Life was for living, not for cowering in the corner like a frightened rabbit.

The image that came to me was the hunter in "The Snows of Kilimanjaro," with his gangrenous leg, waiting stoically, sardonically, for death. It could not have escaped my father. He knew the stories by heart. I was very moved by his courage that evening. He was proud, obstinate, and fatalistic.

Married and with a daughter just born, I needed steady employment. My plays were not selling and I was learning to be a journalist. Living there, working in Fleet Street with English people of all classes, I picked up a lot of their idiom.

It took me a long time to unsquare myself from the influences of family, home, schools, naval expectations. It was easy enough to go my own way professionally and socially, a lot harder to throw off my rather formal speech. I never really did, and both of my brothers still have it. It was easier to write informally than to speak, so indelible was the imprint.

My conditioning probably made it inevitable that when I did

fall into the vernacular and feel at ease, it was in England. I lived there for sixteen years, and it took many of them to adjust my focus to reality. At first I could not escape the feeling that I was walking around in scenery designed by Milne or Thackeray, Shakespeare or Dickens—an emotional reality often stronger than my feelings about the real life of London going on around me.

Some Canadians and Australians I knew in London adopted English speech, accent and all. I did not, although my speech was certainly modified by so much exposure to the rhythms and inflections of the English voice.

Many Canadians of my generation were quite happy to slough off their Canadianism like an unneeded skin. Canadian speech seemed of no more value than Canadian settings for the books and plays we were all in a fever to write. *Real* books were set somewhere else. The trade thought so, as well as the writers. When Hugh MacLennan wrote *Barometer Rising,* a novel about the World War I Halifax explosion, a New York agent asked whether he could set it somewhere else—like an American city. MacLennan is reported to have said once, "Boy meets girl in Winnipeg, and who cares?" It took another generation to realise that Canada and Canadians were material as fertile as anything else. Canada's painters discovered that before her writers, so the tortured birth of a Canadian psychic identity happened first visually, then in letters.

I deceived myself into thinking that acquiring English idiom gave me access as a writer to English subject matter. I poured my energies into plays about English people. They were already familiar from the books I had known since childhood, and they had the received glamour of all those literary echoes. That made them a lot more interesting to me than Canadians, who had no literary echoes whatsoever. And London was the most fascinating place I could imagine. Who needed provincial Canada? It took me about thirty years to think differently.

Now I suspect that if I had not cut myself off from my cultural roots, the creative writing might have gone better. Your language is your culture, your most intimate possession outside your secrets.

I feel that way when I go back to Halifax now, because that is really where the words came from. The books may have been written in England, but the sensibility which absorbed them was formed in Halifax, and there I acquired a feeling for words.

As I advanced professionally and became more confident personally, my style became an amalgam of English, American, and Canadian idiom—like my spelling, an incorrigible mixture. As that happened I found another source of pleasure in the language: I became a collector of expressions and pronunciations that tickled me wherever I travelled—Cockney, Scots, Irish, Lancashire, upper-class English, African, West Indian, Australian, Brooklynese, Yiddish, Southern, Texan, and so on. To this day my informal speech is a pastiche of pieces of vernacular acquired here and there. I like the British expression *putting the cat among the pigeons,* so I use it, as I do the Yiddish *schlep* and *kvetch.* I use the Canadian *eh?* and *bye for now,* the Texan *dippy* and *dipshit,* the Scots *dinna fret yourself,* and the Cockney *wotcha, mate?* because they are funny in the right places. The roots of all this eclecticism reach back to my childhood, when the way people spoke differentiated them for me as vividly as their looks.

I noticed and repeated the little speech eccentricities of my family and their friends. My grandfather Dr. Oxner said *a great deal* as *graydeal* and referred to the place he kept his car as the *garridge,* to rhyme with *carriage,* whereas my mother said *garahj.* His wife, Daisy, the lady from Chattanooga, became noticeably more *Southren,* as my mother called it, at social gatherings when she was the center of attention. She would perch on the edge of her chair, sipping her tea or sherry, occasionally puffing inexpertly on a cigarette. As her eyes sparkled, I noticed that her vowels would lengthen; her usually quick and impatient "Yes, dear? yes, dear? yes, dear?" would become a longer "Yes, deah?"—soft and drawn out.

In my other grandmother's house in Montreal was an old woman, Hattie Parker, who had come from Ireland as a teenage orphan to be a servant to my great-grandmother. By the time I knew her, she was in her eighties, a tiny wrinkled creature with huge dark eyes in a face like a pale walnut and with a bun of white hair. In those seventy years in Montreal she had kept all her Irishness, full of forebodings and superstitions. She sat in a windowseat in a highnecked black dress, nibbling a bit of thread to make it go through her needle, stroking her dress over her knees, muttering disapproval of the neighbours passing in the street. Over the years, my grandmother Emily MacNeil had picked up Hattie's expressions; so had my father and so did I. They were part of the family language, used mockingly, affectionately, yet with a slight exaggeration in tone that indicated you were quoting Hattie.

The back o' me hand to you . . . I'll have none of your lip now . . . The truth isn't in him . . . It'll be the death of me . . . May the saints preserve us . . . Mary and Joseph, did you ever see the like of that? . . . It'd try the patience of a saint.

I heard more English accents. The Canadian Navy had many former British officers, and they were my parents' friends during the war—one family in particular, the Prentices. Captain Prentice looked like a cartoonist's idea of a British sea dog, a square face with thick black eyebrows, one of them clamped down on a monocle. He was a renowned fighting sailor, credited with three U-boat kills. We saw a lot of them, and their son, James, became a close friend. The Prentices spoke with an upper-class English accent, of the type sometimes satirized now as "frightfully-frightfully." My mother loved it. She would say: "They talk so beautifully. I love to hear them talk." I did not end up speaking like James, but my ear caught up with my reading eye, already familiar with British schoolboy expressions, *rath*-ER, *I say chaps, oh, bad luck, top hole, spiffing game,* and so on. Coincidentally, the announcer we most often heard on the BBC was named Prentice, and I found after a while that I had absorbed enough to imitate their accents quite well.

I found amusement in my mother's expressions when she was mildly annoyed: *hells bells!, you imp of satan!, fiddlededee!,* and *fiddlesticks!* The last has a long history, back to Shakespeare at least, meaning literally a bow for a fiddle, or a sword, or what nonsense! Also, according to Eric Partridge's *Dictionary of Slang and Unconventional English,* it has a bawdy meaning, obvious if you think of it.

My father's expletives, probably from Hattie Parker, were *Jesus wept!* or *Jesus, Murphy,* or, slipping out of a room if he was being nagged, *suffering Christ!*

We had girls from Newfoundland who worked for a few months as maids and moved on. One came from Port aux Basques and spoke with a wonderful twang, full of Irish *r*'s and expressions like *Stay where you're to till I come where you're at.*

Thus I developed a conscious pleasure in hearing different accents and the idiom that went with them.

The CBC carried a weekly radio program from Port of Spain, with Calypso music and commentary. I was fascinated by the

West Indian accents and loved to imitate Lord Caressa and the others, in both the pronunciation and lilting rhythm of their delightful English:

> If you want to be happy
> And lead a good life
> Never make a pre-tty wo-man
> —Your wife.

Travelling as a journalist I delighted in finding pockets of distinctive English, as a botanist is thrilled to discover a new variety of plant. The analogy is good, because varieties of English transplanted produced mutations in their new soil—Australia, Africa, Asia, the Caribbean, and North America.

In London, I revelled in Cockney rhyming slang: *You've got a nice set of Hampsteads* (from Hampstead Heath, which rhymes with teeth) or *Get your trouble a new titfer* (trouble and strife = wife, tit for tat = hat), and the endless supply of bawdy ones like *She's got a fine pair of Bristols* (Bristol City = titty).

I find great pleasure in the intonations and structures of American black English. My colleague Charlayne Hunter-Gault told me recently of going through an airport security check. The black woman attendant looked admiringly at the hat Charlayne was wearing and said, "Girl, you is *wearin'* that hat!"

I rejoiced in expressions I heard from another colleague, Cheryl Gruver, from Carthage, Texas. When Jimmy Carter was running for President, he came to our studio to be interviewed. When he left, Cheryl said, "He's so smooth, he's as smooth as a possum's testicle."

I also developed an early taste for, and some skill in composing, limericks; though I have never equalled one I was told years ago and have not seen in any anthology:

> There was a young lady from Chichester,
> Who made all the saints in their niches stir.
> One morning at Matins,
> Her bosom in satins
> Made the Bishop of Chichester's britches stir.

Thus over the years my pleasure has grown for all varieties of English—classical and contemporary, serious and light, proper and bawdy—and I am amazed when I realise that many people do not know that pleasure.

If a man loves cars, to know him is to know his passion. He talks lovingly of the cars he has owned, shows you pictures, shows you what he owns today, and talks of what he dreams of owning. So it is with people who love wine, or paintings, or old bus station signs.

Who enthuses about English today? Who transmits enthusiasm? Obviously some professionals do: teachers, professors, critics, and writers. But what of the amateurs, those who love English words and phrases the way other people love porcelain or music? I have come to think that sharing and transmitting that pleasure is something the culture does not encourage—in fact, may actively discourage, in the sense of the French origin of the word *décourager:* to take the heart out of it.

Isn't it time to consider the amazing riches we possess? In our small heads, we carry a code to our civilisation that parallels our biological genetic inheritance. The words and syntax of this code plug us into the collective memory of our culture. We may pronounce and use the words differently but we have on our lips and in our brain cells the living DNA, if you like, of our race. It is not transmitted genetically but almost as surely. From the Saxons and beyond, to us across fifteen hundred years, from mother to child, from older children to younger children, the words have passed from lip to ear, from mind to mind. Their houses have disappeared, their paintings have flaked away, their golden objects have been melted down, but their words live in us. Not just their words: English has taken thousands of words from other languages. Four-fifths of our vocabulary is borrowed. So in this vast compendium of words are links to many other cultures.

To be fanciful, English has reconstituted something analogous to the lost parent language from which so much human speech descends into the Indo-European group of languages. Long ago, with the wanderings of the peoples, a common-source language gradually broke down into many branches—the Latin and Romance languages, the German and Slavic, the Greek, Persian, and Indian. Now English has spun many bright threads from those tongues back into a yarn richer and more various than any other living language, and considerably more influential.

If people do not know what they are missing, it is a pity, because this is a time of widespread anxiety about the language. Some Americans fear that English will be engulfed or diluted by Spanish and want to make it the official language. There is anxiety about a crisis of illiteracy, or a crisis of semi-literacy among high school, even college, graduates. There is even anxiety that written English is on the way out. Gore Vidal expresses it elegantly in his introduction to Logan Pearsall Smith's *Trivia:*

> As human society abandoned the oral tradition for the written text, the written culture is now being replaced by the audio

visual one. . . . What is to become of that written language which was for two millennia wisdom's only mold?

Anxiety may have a perverse side effect: experts who wish to "save" the language may only discourage pleasure in it. Some are good-humoured and tolerant of change, others intolerant and snobbish. Language reinforces feelings of social superiority or inferiority; it creates insiders and outsiders; it is a prop to vanity or a source of anxiety, and on both emotions the language snobs play. Yet the changes and the errors that irritate them are no different in kind from those which have shaped our language for centuries. As Hugh Kenner wrote of certain British critics in *The Sinking Island,* "They took note of language only when it annoyed them." Such people are killjoys: they turn others away from an interest in the language, inhibit their use of it, and turn pleasure off.

Change is inevitable in a living language and is responsible for much of the vitality of English; it has prospered and grown because it was able to accept and absorb change.

People are deeply attached to the language they use, more emotionally involved than they may know. I am easily offended when someone questions my pronunciation or usage—and broadcasters are constantly being corrected by the audience. My first emotion is anger, even when it is immediately apparent that I am wrong, because the correction seems to imply an attack on more than one innocent word: not a sniper shot out of the woods but the opening of a siege on my entire education and culture.

In Britain I once interviewed the rightwing politician Enoch Powell, notorious for opposing more black immigration. Powell was a former schoolmaster. When I asked what he *envisaged* happening, he stopped me to say, "I think you mean *envi-*

sioned." I didn't but let it go because the cameras were running. When we stopped, we argued about it. It was humiliating to be corrected in public and infuriating to be told patronisingly that *"envisage* must be a Canadian usage." In fact it was one of many ancient usages that persisted in North America and changed in Britain. That exchange ended up on the cutting-room floor.

As people evolve and do new things, their language will evolve too. They will find ways to describe the new things and their changed perspective will give them new ways of talking about the old things. For example, electric light switches created a brilliant metaphor for the oldest of human experiences, being *turned on* or *turned off*. To language conservatives those expressions still have a slangy, low ring to them; to others they are vivid, fresh-minted currency, very spendable, very *with it*.

That tolerance for change represents not only the dynamism of the English-speaking peoples since the Elizabethans, but their deeply-rooted ideas of freedom as well. This was the idea of the Danish scholar Otto Jespersen, one of the great authorities on English. Writing in 1905, Jespersen said in his *Growth and Structure of the English Language:*

> The French language is like the stiff French garden of Louis XIV, while the English is like an English park, which is laid out seemingly without any definite plan, and in which you are allowed to walk everywhere according to your own fancy without having to fear a stern keeper enforcing rigorous regulations. The English language would not have been what it is if the English had not been for centuries great respecters of the liberties of each individual and if everybody had not been free to strike out new paths for himself.

Robert MacNeil

I like that idea and do not think it just coincidence. Consider that the same cultural soil, the Celtic-Roman-Saxon-Danish-Norman amalgam, which produced the English language also nourished the great principles of freedom and rights of man in the modern world. The first shoots sprang up in England and they grew stronger in America. Churchill called them "the joint inheritance of the English-speaking world." At the very core of those principles are popular consent and resistance to arbitrary authority; both are fundamental characteristics of our language. The English-speaking peoples have defeated all efforts to build fences around their language, to defer to an academy on what was permissible English and what not. They'll decide for themselves, thanks just the same.

Nothing better expresses resistance to arbitrary authority than the persistence of what grammarians have denounced for centuries as "errors." In the common speech of English-speaking peoples—Americans, Englishmen, Canadians, Australians, New Zealanders, and others—these usages persist, despite rising literacy and wider education. We hear them every day:

Double negative: "I don't want none of that."

Double comparative: "Don't make that any more heavier!"

Wrong verb: "Will you learn me to read?"

These "errors" have been with us for at least four hundred years, because you can find each of them in Shakespeare.

Double negative: In *Hamlet,* the King says:

> Nor what he spake, though it lack'd form a little, Was not like madness.

Double comparative: In *Othello,* the Duke says:

> Yet opinion . . . throws a more safer voice on you.

Wrong verb: In *Othello,* Desdemona says:

> My life and education both do learn me how to respect you.

I find it very interesting that these forms will not go away and lie down. They were vigorous and acceptable in Shakespeare's time; they are far more vigorous today, although not acceptable as standard English. Regarded as error by grammarians, they are nevertheless in daily use all over the world by a hundred times the number of people who lived in Shakespeare's England.

It fascinates me that *axe,* meaning *ask,* so common in black American English, is standard in Chaucer in all forms—*axe, axen, axed:* "and *axed* him if Troilus were there." Was that transmitted across six hundred years or simply reinvented?

English grew without a formal grammar. After the enormous creativity of Shakespeare and the other Elizabethans, seventeenth- and eighteenth-century critics thought the language was a mess, like an overgrown garden. They weeded it by imposing grammatical rules derived from tidier languages, chiefly Latin, whose precision and predictability they trusted. For three centuries, with some slippage here and there, their rules have held. Educators taught them and written English conformed. Today, English-language newspapers, magazines, and books everywhere broadly agree that correct English obeys these rules. Yet the wild varieties continue to threaten the garden of cultivated English and, by their numbers, actually dominate everyday usage.

Non-standard English formerly knew its place in the social order. Characters in fiction were allowed to speak it occasionally. Hemingway believed that American literature really did not begin until Mark Twain, who outraged critics by reproducing the vernacular of characters like Huck Finn. Newspapers still clean up the grammar when they quote the ungrammatical, including politicians. The printed word, like Victorian morality, has often constituted a conspiracy of respectability.

People who spoke grammatically could be excused the illusion that their writ held sway, perhaps the way the Normans thought that French had conquered the language of the vanquished Anglo-Saxons. A generation ago, people who considered themselves educated and well-spoken might have had only glancing contact with non-standard English, usually in a well-understood class, regional, or rural context.

It fascinates me how differently we all speak in different circumstances. We have levels of formality, as in our clothing. There are very formal occasions, often requiring written English: the job application or the letter to the editor—the dark-suit, serious-tie language, with everything pressed and the lint brushed off. There is our less formal out-in-the-world language—a more comfortable suit, but still respectable. There is language for close friends in the evenings, on weekends—blue-jeans-and-sweat-shirt language, when it's good to get the tie off. There is family language, even more relaxed, full of grammatical short cuts, family slang, echoes of old jokes that have become intimate shorthand—the language of pyjamas and uncombed hair. Finally, there is the language with no clothes on; the talk of couples—murmurs, sighs, grunts—language at its least self-conscious, open, vulnerable, and primitive.

Broadcasting has democratized the publication of language, often at its most informal, even undressed. Now the ears of the educated cannot escape the language of the masses. It surrounds them on the news, weather, sports, commercials, and the ever-proliferating talk and call-in shows.

This wider dissemination of popular speech may easily give

purists the idea that the language is suddenly going to hell in this generation, and may explain the new paranoia about it.

It might also be argued that more Americans hear more correct, even beautiful, English on television than was ever heard before. Through television more models of good usage reach more American homes than was ever possible in other times. Television gives them lots of colloquial English, too, some awful, some creative, but that is not new.

Hidden in this is a simple fact: our language is not the special private property of the language police, or grammarians, or teachers, or even great writers. The genius of English is that it has always been the tongue of the common people, literate or not.

English belongs to everybody: the funny turn of phrase that pops into the mind of a farmer telling a story; or the travelling salesman's dirty joke; or the teenager saying, "Gag me with a spoon"; or the pop lyric—all contribute, are all as valid as the tortured image of the academic, or the line the poet sweats over for a week.

Through our collective language sense, some may be thought beautiful and some ugly, some may live and some may die; but it is all English and it belongs to everyone—to those of us who wish to be careful with it and those who don't care.

One other reason, I believe, for a lack of conscious pleasure in our language today is a neglect of the spoken word, paradoxical as that may seem in this age of broadcast talk.

It may be that as a culture we are losing our ear because we have consigned good English to the printed page; because we define literature as what is written to be read silently; because we are not judging language with our ears as well as our intelligence. In the torrents of words that drown our culture, have we forgotten how to listen? There is little public speaking that is not reading from a printed text, with prompting devices to give an illusion of spontaneity. Just as we do not require school children and college students to write as much as in the past, so we do not impose on them the habit of listening in the traditional ways. That neglect may be responsible for some of our trouble because it means failing to develop the conscious ear that becomes the unconscious, governing ear.

As we expose more and more people to some form of higher education, they may take literacy so much for granted that when they think of language they think of print, not speech. That disconnection may explain why so many well-educated people do not find pleasure in the mother tongue and why so many use it unbeautifully.

To get it "right" we turn increasingly to computers and smart typewriters. Yet the more we process words electronically, and let computer programs choose our vocabulary, spelling, and syntax, the more disconnected we may become, the more remote from the sound of our language, and therefore from a feeling for the weight of words.*

We are adrift today in a sea of weightless words. As Eliot said, words *will not stay in place;* they float like the astronauts' pencils in space.

* This sentence appeared in a recent book on how word processing may affect writing. "Our concrete proposals for influencing self-transformation at the interface are guided by the broad paradigm of contemplative concentration as found in the discipline called meditation." A reviewer commented: "That means when you work at a computer, it's a good idea to stop and think every now and then."

There must be some living connection between the weight of words and truth—not literal, factual truth, perhaps, but an effort at truth, like the effort of a poet, someone who struggles for truth. Today, it seems, words increasingly mean nothing to the person using them, have no connection to what he believes, yet are presented as though they had.

The public words of public men seem to be used increasingly like aerosol room fresheners, to make nice smells. The President of the United States routinely uttered words he did not think through, words that he had not searched his thoughts to find; just a package of words on a file card. Occasionally he read the wrong set and laughed it off.

The U.S. was founded on words that weighed heavily, words that carried the deepest convictions of thoughtful, daring men. Would you believe a politician today who said he pledged his life and his sacred honour? Or have those words just come to be a way of sounding sincere?

Today we can weigh invisible atomic particles, we can weigh stars so distant man will never reach them, yet we have lost the way of weighing words. Students are seldom obliged to search for words. They are given the different task of selecting from multiple choices, of guessing, of betting odds. If they guess right, they pass; disposable words good only for one test.

Politics, the law, advertising, religion become the art of employing words to cover for the moment, to get you off the hook, to win a verdict, pass a test, fill a space, get rid of a question.

There are antidotes to this poison of weightless words. Any good writer will give you good weight. Often it is only words of fiction which have it. How do writers learn the weight of words? From childhood, they read and are read to; they read more and listen; they listen to the language the way artists look at paintings.

If you love the language, the greatest thing you can do to ensure its survival is not to complain about bad usage but to pass your enthusiasm to a child. Find a child and read to it often the things you admire, not being afraid to read the classics.

Exposing children to the words of the classics will do them no more harm than articulate adults do in conversation. Not to be exposed is not to have the chance of learning. If adults always talked down to them, children might never advance beyond baby talk. There is real deprivation in restricting them to pabulum dished up by someone with a prescribed average of how many words a six-year-old should know; the effect must be to drive the level ever downwards, both in terms of expression and of sentiments.

The children will not be aware of what you are really doing for them. I certainly wasn't aware that it was being done to me. I just liked being read good stories.

All boys can throw once they see another do it and practice a lot. I cannot remember not knowing how. Like the other boys, I threw all the time—baseballs, marbles, stones, acorns, snowballs—at bottles, squirrels, trees, other boys, windows in abandoned houses, and one taxi. If anyone had asked me how the pleasure of being read a poem or story compared with the pleasure of throwing something, there would have been no contest.

Humans have been throwing for thousands of years, perhaps longer than they have been talking or at least using words. Someone who does not try throwing, for example a girl brought up to believe that it is boyish, will not be able to. Innately the talent or capacity is there, the pathways in her brain are there but have not been used, except perhaps to observe boys throwing.

People who do not develop the pathways for words will be

like the girl trying to throw. They have all the innate equipment; the circuitry is built in; only the software and practice are missing. It intrigues me to realise how long the software loading took to produce in me a sense of accomplishment and pleasure with words remotely comparable to what I got instantly from throwing. The words must have been delayed-action devices, planted to explode later.

It was not until many years later that I became consciously aware of the pleasure of words. Yet the seeds were being planted all the time I was learning to throw, ride a bike, swim, skate, and build snow forts.

Eighteen months after they moved to London, my father had a heart attack in Paris. After a long convalesence he went back to work. Then, in November 1959, I got a call saying he had died, of another heart attack, in Athens. He was fifty-three.

The Canadian government shipped his body back to London, and my mother and I went together to see him in the Harrods funeral parlor. The body was in a plain oak coffin with the lid off, but draped with a lace veil. Alone, before others came, we drew it back to look at him.

Death had recomposed his face and made it quite youthful. So much lived life, so much unlived. He wore a hurt expression, his upper lip compressed over the lower. His hands crossed over his body were flat, but the last joint of each finger was curled down. He had not gone gentle into that good night.

My mother was not shy of the man she had been married to for thirty years. She reached into the coffin and felt his chest firmly with her fingers, to feel how solid it was, to confirm something for herself.

It felt strange to be looking at my own father's body through a reporter's eyes, thinking of words that would describe him while experiencing that breathless quality the dead inspire, their chests so still you imagine yours paralysed too.

To his three sons he bequeathed his accomplishments and the things he did not do. It is significant how much of our lives we have spent doing just those things, balancing his account with life. Thus in his fantasies he moves us still. There was plenty of him to go around.

Michael, the youngest, now a computer and management consultant living in Ottawa, loves books, music, and travel.

Hugh not only prospered in the Navy but rose to the very top. At this writing, he is a Vice Admiral and the Deputy Chief of the Defence Staff in Ottawa. He is as avid a reader and book collector as the rest of us.

Our mother returned to Halifax, remarried after ten years, but was again widowed. She is now in her eighties and sturdy, with seven grandchildren. She still loves the sea, flowers, the woods—and reading.

She lives on precisely the spot where we lived during World War II, in an apartment block replacing several of the old wooden houses that still give South Park Street its Victorian character.

From her balcony I can look down on a map of my boyhood fifty years ago. Little has changed. Through the trees I can follow the way I walked to Tower Road School. Below me are the fences I used to teeter along between the gardens whose fruit trees I plundered. When I look up, there is the great harbour, its mouth opening to the Atlantic, through which my father's ships came and went.

Looking down, remembering the incidents of those years, I -

My mother with me in 1983,
at the site of the cottage in Pictou
where we spent the summer
of 1943

think, This is where I was first struck by words. This is where they made me more than a Canadian, an Englishman, or an American; or Scottish, or Irish, or German—all the things my forebears were. This is where I became what Joseph Brodsky calls a "citizen of the great English language."

Postscript

When *Wordstruck* was published, my mother read it at one sitting. She had many telling comments but the most moving was this: "I'm so glad you did this before I set out on my long journey."

Six months later, in August 1989, she died suddenly but peacefully.